To
Armando
&
Nancy

Pedro Escobedo

My Life in the Key of E

My Life in the Key of

E

A Memoir by Pete Escovedo
With Sarah Spinner Escovedo, Psy.D.

Interior design by Rony Armas
Jacket design by Rony Armas
Cover photography © Carl Studna

Manufactured in the United Sates of America

ISBN 978-0-692-87885-9

All insert photographs are courtesy of the author unless otherwise noted.

DEDICATION

I hope that the tales within these pages will allow my family members to gain a greater understanding of who it is that they call husband, father, brother, in-law, cousin, uncle, grandfather, great-grandfather, musician, and artist. I have a sense that my main purpose in telling this story—my central message—has to do with the importance of family. And so I dedicate this book to mine.

A special dedication to my parents, Pedro B. Escovedo and Anita Valenzuela, who started me on this journey, and to the loves of my life: Juanita ("Moms"), Sheila ("Cho"), Juan ("J.E."), Peter Michael ("Peto"), and Zina ("Dink").

TABLE OF CONTENTS

ACKNOWLEDGMENTS

Thank you to my Lord, Jesus Christ, for this miracle and gift of life, for the beautiful moments I've lived so far, and for all the music I've been able to play.

Thank you to my family (the Escovedos, Garderes, Chevereses, and Quesadas) for the unconditional love, support, laughter, and for giving my life meaning. Thank you to my fans—who are both friends and extended family—for the nonstop support.

Thank you to my daughter-in-law Dr. Sarah Spinner Escovedo for so skillfully and lovingly helping me to tell my story.

Thank you to my many dear friends who have stayed by my side and traveled with me on this wild journey, supporting me in all my endeavors (and helping me set up and break down my timbales!) along the way. They've been there from the beginning, through the ups and downs, for the downbeats and the bows: Al Larios, Bobby "Choco" Ochoa, Don Kaneshige, Henry Royal, the "Rat Pack Boys"–

Joe Baez, J.T. Torres, Chino, Rick "Ricky Boy" Kemp, Xavier Christy, and Johnny Mac.

Special shout-out to Val Nunes for his inspiring philanthropy, his extraordinarily generous heart, and being such a wonderful friend.

Thank you to Jason Hofmann for his friendship, support, and generosity.

Thank you to Rony Armas for his excellent book-layout and design skills.

Thank you to Elizabeth Spinner and Brenda Vaccaro, Psy.D., for their love of language and eye for detail.

Thank you to the Behring family for their friendship and for displaying my painting *Chief Yellow Feather* in the Blackhawk Museum.

Thank you to my past and present endorsees, who made my playing easier and better: Toca/LP Pete Escovedo Signature Timbales, Zildjian Cymbals, Remo Timbale Heads, Vic Firth Timbale Sticks, and Gibraltar Cymbal Stands.

An extra special thanks to my manager, Victor Pamiroyan, who always has my back and my best interest at heart.

And to every musician I've had the pleasure of recording with, sharing music with, or just hanging out with, thank you for blessing me with your time and your talent. *Gracias amigos.*

INTRODUCTION

SCORING MY LIFE ON PAGES

October 18, 2012
5 p.m.
Valley Glen, California

Here I am, at my desk, trying to write an introduction to my book. I've wanted to write a memoir for a long time, but I wasn't sure how to put all the pieces together. There've been so many opening acts, finales, intermissions, and lots of encores. There's been some improvisation, some swing, some syncopation, some blues, and lots of high notes. Like jazz music, my life story, and even the writing of this book, have felt pretty unpredictable.

A few days ago, I came back from playing some gigs in my old stomping grounds, the San Francisco Bay Area. Los Angeles is where I live now, but the Bay Area will always feel most like home. Today has been slow-moving and rainy. Not much to do on a day like this, I thought, so I came into my office to try and finish this book.

I started this project a few years ago, trying my best to remember and piece together my life from day one to today. I like writing song lyrics, but writing this book has been nothing like that. I can create storylines to fit a song, but I don't write the actual music itself. And writing a book feels like trying to write out an entire symphony–all the different instruments, structures, and melodic changes. This is like scoring my life on pages.

In quiet moments–which are pretty rare in my house–I've had flashes of my life go through my mind like streaks of lightning across the sky. How do I capture all those moments that matter? Well, here goes my attempt.

I think each person's life has a main story. There's the "when" and the "where," of course, and then there are all the moments worth recording–the stuff that happens to us by chance and the stuff we choose, whether they're good or bad choices in the end. And there are all the people who have shaped our lives. Finally, there's the message we want to leave behind, the message that will live on, even when the story ends. My message, I believe, is about the importance of family, in all its many forms.

CHAPTER ONE

DAWN-THE BEGINNING

My Father
Pedro Barrera Escobedo
Born September 15, 1906
Saltillo, Mexico

My father's own life story, particularly his early life, remains almost entirely inaccessible to me. It's a scattered tale that's been handed down through quiet whispers, confident assertions, and pure speculation. What I "know" of his early years is equal parts truth, rumor, and mystery. He was one of three or four children. He was an only son, with two or three sisters. And his father and mother, my grandparents, are people I never met.

My mother's younger sister, Aunt Tomasa ("Tommy"), and my sister Jay have told me bits and pieces of my dad's life. They remember how handsome he was, how charming, how full of fun. But uncles on my mother's side didn't seem to like him too much. During the few times I heard them talk about him, it usually wasn't positive. "He's no good, that one," they'd say. But they wouldn't offer any specifics. And many years later, his second wife, Cleo, who I now call "Mom" since it feels fitting to me, filled in a few of the lingering blanks. But even she didn't have a lot of answers. It seems easier for folks to talk about his essence than to provide any facts.

Cleo did tell me that he ran away from home when he was about 15. Apparently his parents blamed him for his sister's death. He'd been running after her in the streets, during what should've been an innocent game of chase, when she was struck by a passing car. His parents could never forgive him for being there, for being part of this unthinkable tragedy. I don't know how true any of this is. But I've been told that soon after that, my dad, stricken with guilt and grief and unable to bear his parents constantly blaming him, boarded a ship in Mexico and headed for Alaska. Did he work on the ship? Was he a stowaway? What did he do when he got to Alaska, and how long did he stay there? I know none of these answers or if this part of his story is even true. I only know that eventually he ended up in San Francisco, California.

How did he get there? What did he do there? How did he make a living? How old was he? Again, I have no answers. But I believe this is where he met my mother.

My Mother
Anita Valenzuela
Born December 28, 1911
San Francisco, California

My mother's story, while a lot clearer than my father's, is interwoven with some mystery too. I've gathered bits and pieces, but I've never quite grasped how each piece created a whole. I know that my grandmother Luisa Saldanea had two sons and three daughters: Uncle George, Uncle Manuel,

Aunt Angelina ("Jiggs"), Aunt Tommy, and my mother. My aunts and uncles all had different last names, I guess because my grandmother had a few husbands. I never knew my biological grandfather, but my grandmother's last husband, a very kind soul named James, who we all called Jamos, was the only grandfather I ever knew. My grandparents lived in Pittsburg, California, which would be my birthplace. Grandfather Jamos worked at the Dow Chemical plant along with Uncle George and Uncle Manuel.

When my parents married, my father was 22 and my mother was just 17. My dad didn't have much of an education and Mom, being so young, had very little schooling herself. I'm not sure she even finished high school. So making a living was not easy. Farm work was the only kind of consistent employment they could find. Unable to afford a place of their own, they stayed in the housing shacks used by the farmworkers and their families. Each season they traveled around California, picking fruit in the fields day after day. It's all this travel that explains why each of their kids was born in a different small California town.

My parents' first born was a girl who died as a baby, her life cut short by whooping cough. I never knew her name or how old she was when she died. My mother didn't talk about losing her baby, and I didn't find out until I was an adult. It was one of many bits of family history that I learned about so many years later. There were a lot of secrets on both sides of my family, and sometimes I wonder which ones are still uncovered, which ones are still actively protected, and which ones will stay forever buried.

I might have heard, or maybe imagined hearing, that my dad wasn't there when my sister died. I think about my mother carrying that memory alone for so many years. Sometimes I wonder how she got through that emotional loss, or if she ever did. My father may have been out on one of his drunken binges when it happened. I have only flashes of memory about this. Again, when it comes to my father, details exist in a blurry space between truth and fiction.

My oldest brother, Manuel, was born December 30, 1929; my sister Jessie, who we call "Jay," was born on Christmas day, December 25, 1930; and my other sister, Alice, shared the same birthday as Manuel, December 30, in 1932. And then there was me: Peter Michael Escovedo, born on July 13, 1935, in Pittsburg, California. My brother Robert (Bobby) was born November 4, 1938. And our youngest sibling, my brother Thomas, was born on April 30, 1940. Aunt Tommy gave Thomas the nickname "Coke" because he loved drinking Coca Cola in those little glass bottles. They called me "Mico" because some of the kids misheard when the older relatives were calling me *"Mijo"* (little son). Somehow the wrong name stuck. (It's like how when my kids were young they heard their cousins calling me *"Tio,"* which is Spanish for "Uncle." My kids misheard it as "Theo," and so that nickname has stuck.) By this time, my father had changed his last name from Escobedo to Escovedo. I'm not sure when or why the decision was made for the "b" to become a "v."

My parents had a hard time raising a large family, working tireless days in the fields, and traveling from town to town–their schedules and whereabouts dependent entirely on where the picking jobs were. We kids joined them on the fields, picking and boxing lettuce, oranges, cherries, and nuts. The days were long and hot. When I was little, I figured all kids must spend their days on these farms. But as I grew older, I learned that wasn't the case. And by the time I was a teenager, I dreaded spending my summers out there in the relentless heat. I was dreaming of another life. *I can't do this forever*, I'd think. *There's got to be another way.*

Eventually, they grew tired of all the travel and decided it was time to settle in one place, back in the small town where I was born, Pittsburg, California. For employment, they were solely dependent on chemical plants like Dow.

One time, it seemed like all my parents' hard work was paying off. Our house on Black Diamond Street was the first one that was big enough to hold all of us. It had a big yard with one large tree in the middle. We'd chase each other around that tree to the point of exhaustion before collapsing onto the soft grass beneath us, belly-laughing, and staring up to the sky. But we didn't get to play around the tree for long, as it was soon time to move again. We kept going from little house to little house. Usually the kids shared a bedroom. Sometimes, if we were lucky, our parents were in one room, the girls in their own, and the boys in another. But that was rare.

My dad must've realized that without a trade, work would continue to be hard to find. So he put himself through night school, eventually becoming a qualified pipe fitter, a job for which there was high demand since it was wartime–World War II–and men were needed to build naval ships. It was this new army base job that would take us to the most important geographical backdrop of my life: Oakland, California. We had to practice air raid drills when they sounded the alarm, lowering all the window shades and ducking. I lived in fear of it one day being real, not just a practice run, and I wondered if I'd be able to keep my cool if the Japanese finally decided to drop the bomb on Oakland. Women also were called to help with the war effort, and so my mother went to work in the plants and factories. She'd come home in her overalls, and I'd ask her about what she did on the assembly line that day.

"The same as yesterday, Peter," she'd say. I could tell she was tired.

She had a drawer filled with ration coupons for purchasing hard to get items like sugar and meat, gasoline, and car tires. I was told these were given to families in the armed forces. I understood that there was a shortage of some kind and that resources were scarce, so I felt sort of special, knowing that my parents had earned these rare coupons.

⚜

My father continued working at the army and navy base, day in and day out, for about three years. But things were about to change for him and my mom. His love of music, and his burning desire to sing, led him to dance halls and night clubs where he'd often join in with the musicians for a song or two. After the show, he'd invite them all back to our house to continue the fun. We always had the makings for a great party—lots of food, lots of drink, and lots of music. He loved the good times, the joy of being around creative souls, and the delight of sharing music. He'd proudly belt out his favorite Mexican songs like *Solamente Una Vez*. He'd sing that one a lot, in Spanish and in English. "Only once I loved. Only once and never more...."

We began to see that his love of music went right along with his love of drinking. They both became habits he couldn't stop. While the music, in and of itself, seemed to be a happy escape, his drinking was a dark one. Eventually, it turned him into a completely different person—from jovial and fun-loving to cynical and angry. My mother began to send us kids along with him whenever he went to the dance hall, particularly for the Sunday *tardeadas* where kids were allowed. It's not like our presence stopped him from drinking, but maybe it slowed him down a bit. I guess our mother knew that our rolling-stone father would be more likely to come home when we were tagging along.

Sometimes, since kids weren't allowed most places, we'd sit in the car parked outside whichever ballroom or music venue Dad had chosen that night—Sweet's, the Ali Baba, the Sands. We'd roll down the car windows and listen to the sweet sounds of the Dorsey Brothers, Count Basie, Machito, and Perez Prado. Dad especially loved the big bands, and he'd make sure they followed us back to our house for an after-party that lasted until morning.

Other times, we'd wait by the side door of the dance hall, peeking in to get a better glimpse. I wanted to get closer to the sound. My eyes would dart back and forth between my father and the stage. He'd be drinking at the bar, twirling women around the dance floor, and by the end of the night, sitting in with the band. I liked watching him on stage–his smile lighting up his whole face, his feet tapping to the sounds of the big orchestra, the music enveloping his body. By watching my father indulge in his musical escapes, music was becoming more and more a part of me too.

But Dad's excursions weren't just about music. They were increasingly about drinking, which meant they were about getting out and staying out. He'd cash his paycheck and head straight for the nearest bar, sometimes not returning home for days. When my mother figured out which bar he was holed up in, she'd send one or two of us to fetch him and drag him home. Sometimes, when we'd managed to convince him to get off whatever bar stool he'd landed on, we had to actually carry him home. Grown men are heavy. Drunk grown men are even heavier. As hard as it was when he was missing–watching my mother cry, her anger coming out in her loud, pacing footsteps, her harsh voice tone, and her furrowed brows–it was even harder when we had to fetch him and take him home. We knew that once we managed to drag him through the door, there'd be some awful fighting ahead. They'd fight about the paycheck he'd traded in for alcohol, his selfish disappearing acts, and his never-ending need for the bottle. These fights got more and more frequent, and more and more explosive.

One night, while Coke was sound asleep in our shared room, I stared out the window onto the dark streets. Dad had been gone three days, and we'd had no luck finding him. I was sleepless, wondering when–if–he'd be back. And then I saw a figure exiting the bar right across the street and stumbling toward the house. As he got closer, I was instantly relieved. It was him. But he looked all jacked up–wrinkled clothes, messed up hair, off balance. Then, for some reason, he turned around and went back into the bar. When he came out again, just a few minutes later, he was yelling at two guys, picking some kind of fight about God knows what. I watched those two guys beat the mess out of my father before he fell to the ground. I wondered if he was still alive. After what felt like forever, he managed to get himself up and make it inside our house, where he now had to face my mother. He was drunk, beaten up, and had spent his paycheck again. She was livid, screaming and cussing so loud I had to shield Coke's ears.

As they say, alcohol is a cruel mistress. And my mother grew tired of trying to compete with this seductive object of his affection. After 17 years of marriage, she filed for divorce. I was about seven at the time. I didn't know then what this would mean for our family, or how it would lead to even more dramatic changes. I just knew I loved my father, and I couldn't understand why he kept choosing alcohol over my mother, over us. But he was a lost soul–still that outcast boy–trying to survive in a world he wasn't prepared to navigate. He escaped emotional hardship in Mexico, arrived in America with big dreams, married young, and quickly started a family. He tried to provide for us while also trying to numb his many layers of pain. He found some solace in music and liquor. And then he lost everything in a pool of liquid fantasy. I wasn't a witness for the next phase of his life. After leaving us, he began another story, with another family.

While I'm sure my father's leaving brought my mother some relief–no more sleepless nights wondering when he'd come home, if he was alive, if he'd drunk up every cent of his paycheck–it also brought her new struggles. She was suddenly single with six young children to care for. She found work each summer at the Del Monte Cannery in Emeryville, and for the rest of the year worked as a waitress at a café down the street. That must have been where she met Joe. I hated that man. He wasn't my father. And he came around too soon. Sometimes I wondered if he'd been in the picture while my parents were still together. I knew my dad and mom had made each other unhappy, but I still wanted them together. This Joe-guy was just in the way. I didn't trust him, and I got the feeling that he was taking advantage of my mother in every possible way.

When my dad left, the music went with him. Occasionally my mom had big band music on the radio, and she played a little piano here and there. But there were no more trips to the dance halls and no more musicians hanging around the house. So while I still thought about music, I spent more time getting into painting and drawing. There was also a lot less Spanish around me. Dad spoke Spanish a lot more than my mom, so when he left, I barely heard the language. That's why I never became fluent. Only Bobby and Alice would become fluent in Spanish, since they eventually stayed with our Spanish-speaking grandparents. Much later, my inability to speak Spanish fluently would bother me, especially when meeting some of my favorite Spanish-speaking musicians. I wished I could have deeper conversations with them in their native language.

My brother Manuel had joined the Air Force and was stationed in Texas, and since Mom realized she just couldn't afford to care for all of her other kids at once, Alice and Bobby went to live with her mother and Jamos, back in Pittsburg, California. Jay and Coke and I stayed with my mom in a tiny two-room flat on the corner of Seventh Street in Oakland, right above Savelli's Drug Store. My mom and Jay shared a bed in the first room, while in the other room, Coke and I shared a small cot next to the stove. In other words, my brother and I slept in the kitchen. We had to share a bathroom and a shower with all the other tenants. Our little place was filthy, and the smell of urine carried all the way down the hallway from the communal bathroom. Eventually, after Jay moved out to start her new family, it was just me, Coke, and our mother. I already felt like I had close to nothing–not much food, very few clothes, no toys. And now even family members seemed to be slipping away.

CHAPTER TWO

(ARA DE SU PADRE

Occasionally, without much notice or fanfare, parts of the family got to reconnect. One summer, when I was about nine, my mother took me, Coke, and my sister Jay to Mexico to visit Bobby and Alice at our grandparents'–my grandmother, Luisa, who we called "Abuelita" (which is like "granny" in Spanish), and her husband, Jamos. Our mother hadn't seen them since they'd all moved from Pittsburg to Monterey, Mexico. It had to be a tough decision for her to make–allowing two of her children to move to another country–but she was struggling to provide for all of us, and she needed her parents' support. My grandparents had been dead set on moving to Mexico with big plans of opening a bar/restaurant. They'd already sold their home and were ready to invest in this new business venture. Alice and Bobby could attend a good school there, and our grandparents loved taking care of them. And so, after weighing her very limited options, she decided it was the only way.

We traveled by bus, the cheapest way possible. It was a long and tiring journey with many stops before we finally ended up in Nuevo Leon, by the city of Monterey. We dragged our bags to an area just off the highway leading to Mexico City, where my grandparents had set up their establishment, complete with their living quarters in back. It was great to see Alice and Bobby again. Alice was attending college in Mexico which was a big deal. We were all so proud of her for pursuing a higher education. Bobby was eager to hang out with me, but it took some getting used to for both of us. He'd make fun of me trying to speak Spanish, and I'd make fun of him trying to speak English.

We got to explore the surrounding area, but home base was my grandparents' restaurant. I was so impressed to see real customers eating and drinking there. I couldn't believe my grandparents were real business owners who cleverly set things up so that they could live and work on the same property. They seemed to be doing pretty well, welcoming a steady stream of customers who stopped by on their way to or from the city, as well as lots of local Mexican cowboys who would stop by for beers. Jamos loved to join them at the bar, though that never went over well with Abuelita.

I enjoyed watching everybody–Jamos and Abuelita fussing about his drinking, customers stopping in for some refreshments, and mostly, the cowboys. I'd never seen real cowboys before. I'd figured they were just characters from movies and TV. This one cowboy, a regular, would always ride his horse right up to the restaurant, order a beer, and then drink it on the bench out front. One time, I saw another cowboy come up on a horse and stand next to the regular. Then a car raced up, and a third guy got out, staring hard at the two cowboys. They stared back. This didn't look like a friendly staring contest. One of the cowboys finally spoke up. Loudly. "What are you looking at?"

Suddenly, as if that one question was some universal queue, all three of them pulled out their pistols. I couldn't believe what was happening. I felt like I was in an old Western movie. But this was real. In technicolor. The cowboy on the bench shot his pistol, just grazing the driver's ear. The driver jumped into his car and sped off, leaving drops of deep-red blood on the dusty ground. I thought this would be a one-time thing. But I was wrong. It seemed like everyone carried a pistol. Guys were getting loud and crazy out front just about every day. And they were shooting their guns in the air like it was no big deal. My grandmother would holler for us to come to the back whenever she realized we were hanging around these wild cowboys. But I wanted to stay, equally scared and intrigued.

Bull fighting, the big sport there, was something else I felt both scared and intrigued about. One time, Jamos brought us to a real live bull fight, and I couldn't believe what I was seeing. That poor bull. And those daring men. I didn't know what was more dangerous–a pistol or a bull. Playing around with either seemed like a dumb idea. Even though I knew it was dumb, I couldn't help but take my turn as a bull fighter. Jamos had a baby bull tied up in the back, and after I saw the fight, I was inspired to bring out a red napkin from the restaurant and try to tease him, pretending I was a big tough bull fighter. Good thing that little bull was tied up.

Since my mother had to go back to the states to work, she left Jay and me there and took Coke back with her. I figured she'd come back a few days later, but we ended up staying the whole summer. I didn't know it then, but soon, waiting just a summer for my mom would seem like nothing compared to the biggest wait of my life.

⋘⋙

Even though I was missing my mother, I let myself have fun. It felt like an actual vacation–exploring the fields, riding the horses, and swimming under the warm Mexican sun. We felt special getting to swim in a real pool built by Jamos, instead of having to swim where the locals swam, down at the creek where women beat and scrubbed their clothes with small rocks before rinsing them in the fresh water. Every day was filled with adventure, laughter, and moments of just hanging out–happily doing nothing at all. We were so far away from that two-room flat in Oakland.

It took a while to get used to my grandparents, my new temporary caregivers. Jamos was a very quiet, slender man. He was my grandmother's third–maybe fourth– husband. He did all the cooking and managed most of the upkeep at their restaurant. My grandmother stayed busy helping to run the place too. She was a strong woman, and even though they shared the business, I got the feeling she had the last word.

She had the last word with me too. Abuelita was stern, strict, and old-school. It was clear from the beginning that she didn't like me. I looked too much like my dad, who she could never forgive for his bad behavior and for leaving my mom. So every time I passed her, she'd slap me. I tried to duck when I passed. *"Cara de su Padre,"* she'd call me. ("Face of your father.") She'd say it right before the slap. After a while, I just got used to it. I hated it, but I got used to it. I also had to get used to how unfair things seemed. Bobby could do no wrong. Whenever I went out to play with him, I had to be extra careful because if he got dirty or hurt, Abuelita blamed me. "Robertito," she'd call him. And "little angel." And sometimes even "Little Lord Robertito." I worried that she was turning him into a spoiled brat. I was so grateful that my sister Jay was there to take care of me and look out for me. She saw the unfair treatment, and she did her best to protect me. By the end of the summer, I couldn't wait for my mom to come get us. I missed her a lot. And my grandmother's constant slaps were getting to be too much. It didn't make any sense. I didn't ask to have my father's face.

There were lots of things that confused me that summer. I didn't understand all the gun-shooting. I didn't know how long I'd have to stay in Mexico. And, most upsetting of all, I didn't understand why my father left us. I wondered whether or not I'd ever get to see him again. I'd heard he was living in San Antonio, Texas, which could have been as far as Mars for all I knew. I have only one short and hazy memory of Coke and me being in San Antonio with our dad. I think one of his sisters may have taken us, but I'm not sure. We were visiting one of his relatives in a very dark and poorly built house. There were dirt floors and only a few pieces of furniture–a dust-covered chair and a chipped shelf. There was an old person on a cot, and my dad asked me to wait outside so he could speak to this person. "Maybe this is how my father lives," I thought. "Maybe he's dirt-poor and maybe he grew up even poorer than we did."

One night toward the end of the summer marked the worst of my time in Mexico. Abuelita often had Jamos drive her and Alice into the city so they could do some shopping. Whenever she went to the city, Abuelita would tell him, in no uncertain terms, that he was not to drink when they were away. But by the time Abuelita called him to be picked up, he was usually pretty buzzed. And sometimes, having lost track of time in his drunken haze, he wouldn't even notice the phone ringing. When Abuelita called enough times, yelling at him to hurry up, Jamos would shove me and Bobby into the car and speed along the highway toward the city. The "highway" was really nothing more than a two-lane road with very little visibility, so it was pretty important to drive with caution, especially if you had ten beers under your belt. On this night, a horse and a wagon full of men who seemed to have been celebrating as much as Jamos, darted across the highway, right in front of us. We hit the horse first, and it rolled right over the front hood of our car, breaking the windshield. We skidded off the road, missing a large tree by only a few inches before screeching to an abrupt stop. The men jumped off the wagon and scattered in different directions, leaving us and the horse on the bloody road.

When the police finally showed up, they checked us over and told us how lucky we were to only have a few cuts. Bobby looked pale, and I was still shaking, unable to stop staring at the poor horse's body. I couldn't believe how quickly such a healthy creature, full of life and spirit, could become a dead mass in the middle of a road. I loved animals. Knowing that I was in a car that had just killed such a beautiful one was too much for my little mind to handle. Just then, a bus from the city passed us by, and through the window we saw Abuelita and Alice. It seemed like they passed us in slow motion. Abuelita's face was full of hate. Jamos was in deep doo-doo.

I had nightmares after that. And I was afraid of being in cars. Whenever we drove on dark roads, I'd feel my heart beating faster and I could only breathe short, shallow breaths. Finally, my mom came back to get us. Thank goodness. We had worn out our welcome, and even if our home in Oakland was a tiny hole in the wall without access to a pool, horses, or wide open landscapes, I couldn't wait to get back.

CHAPTER THREE

THE "SPECIAL PLACE"

I'd been anxious to get back, but once we walked inside our little apartment above Savelli's Drug Store, I was saddened all over again. It seemed smaller and gloomier than ever. I was growing tired of what seemed like a very tiny world–not much to see and nothing new to listen to. At night, the Pachuco gangs would gather below our house, wearing their leather jackets, each with a tattooed cross between their thumbs and forefingers. I figured they were like the Oakland version of those Mexican cowboys outside my grandparents' restaurant. When I got bored, I'd listen to them from the window–shouting about women, booze, and fighting. I covered Coke's ears so he couldn't hear their nonsense.

"I got that girl last night!"

"Give me that bottle of whiskey!"

"I'm gonna mess you up man!"

During the day, I did my best to find fun outdoors, taking Coke to the park by the police station to play baseball, basketball, or volleyball. Wherever I went, Coke was by my side. He was my responsibility and he loved tagging along. One year, my mom found us a camp for "underprivileged" (i.e., poor) kids. We were excited. Coke would always be by my side there too, even when I was hanging out with the older campers. One day, the kids made a rope swing under a bridge over a river. For some reason, the camp counselors were nowhere in sight. "Go for it, Peter," the kids cheered. "Take a swing." On my first try, I didn't swing hard enough, so I couldn't get to the other side. I was just hanging above the water and had no idea what to do. "Just let go and fall into the water," one of them yelled. I figured I didn't have much choice, so I let go. But the water was deeper than I'd expected and I didn't know how to swim. I was drowning, yelling "Help! Help!" Every time I came up for air, I could see them laughing. They must've thought I was joking–pretending to be in trouble. The only one not laughing was Coke. He could see the fear in my face. Luckily, at just that moment, some people happened to be coming down the river in a canoe, and they scooped me up. I've been nervous about water ever since. I'm fine in a pool, as long as I can get to the shallow end if need be. But you're not going to find me in a river or an ocean any time soon.

Despite some fun times at the park or at camp, life continued to feel pretty strained. There wasn't much new from day to day, and Mom seemed to be getting more and more frustrated with the daily grind. I was realizing how poor we were, and how hard life was for our family. Our home began to feel suffocating, as if the floors and walls and ceilings were creeping in on us. And they seemed to be lined with a dingy layer of despair. For my mother, even this life would soon become impossible to afford. I didn't know how much things were about to change for all of us, how much more I would learn about broken families and broken hope. I didn't know that I'd soon be longing for this home–any home, really.

Nights were long. Coke and I tried to find ways to entertain ourselves. Most nights we'd sit on our little shared cot, stare out the window, and wait for cool cars to speed by below us. "That one's mine," I'd shout, pointing to a shiny hot rod. "No, it's mine," Coke would yell. "I saw it first!" Convertibles were the best ones to claim. We spent hours waiting to see the coolest Fords, Lincolns, Oldsmobiles, and Buicks. The shinier the better. We didn't know that our last night of claiming cars would be our last night there, in a real home, with our mother. It just seemed like any other night. But the next morning, our mother told us to get all our things together.

"I'm taking you to a really special place," she told us.
Coke looked up to her. "Where mom?"
"It's a surprise."

She was using words that sounded happy. But something in her eyes looked sad. As I packed up my clothes, I studied her face. She was rushed, distracted. I wanted to believe that the surprise would be a good one. I liked the idea of another adventure, another trip. And anywhere would be better than this cramped place. I was curious about this "special place," thinking that as long as it wasn't back to Mexico–the scene of that horrible accident–it had to be better than our little apartment.

My mom and her boyfriend, Joe, drove us across the Richmond/San Rafael Bridge. It was the last time I'd ever see Joe. After exiting off the freeway, we headed down a long tree-lined road. First I caught a glimpse of a chapel and then a huge building, shaped like the letter "U," wrapped around a large courtyard. I'd soon learn that this was a place where children lived–older boys on the right and younger boys on the left. I'd learn this because I would stay on the right and Coke would stay on the left. This "special place" turned out to be Saint Vincent's Home for Boys, a place where orphans and foster kids stayed because they had no real home. Our mother led us inside the office where the priest and sisters greeted us. As they began showing us around, my mother tried to make it seem like a fun occasion. "What a nice place you'll be staying at. It's beautiful, isn't it?" I nodded and smiled, because I knew that's what my mother needed.

Then she started to cry. She explained that she was leaving us there because she needed to go back to Mexico to visit Alice and Bobby. "This will only be for a short time, boys. I'll come back and get you real soon." Coke burst into tears.

"I'll watch out for Coke," I told her. "I promise." I forced my tears away as I watched her car get smaller and smaller. I'd never felt so alone. I'd never felt so sad. I put my arms around my crying brother, whose sobs were heavy. His tears were staining my shirt. "Don't cry, Coke." I wiped his face with my shirt sleeve. "She'll be back for us real soon." Then her car disappeared into the trees.

They took Coke to the younger boys' side immediately. He kept turning back to me with his wide brown eyes. "Don't cry!" I yelled to him. "I'll see you soon." Then they led me to the older boys' dormitory. "No," a sister told me in a serious voice. "You won't see your brother soon. Don't focus on him. Your job is to go to school and work in the kitchen. You'll see him on Wednesday movie nights."

I did see him Wednesday nights. And at the pool on warm days. I gave him chocolate bars and packs of gum that I'd bought at the commissary with dollars I'd received in the mail from family members. I spent most of my money on candy and gum for my brother. I couldn't give him much hope, and I couldn't seem to stop his tears, but at least I could bring him treats. The only good thing about my kitchen job was that I could steal cookies to sneak to my brother the next time I saw him.

Nighttime was hard. The boys' beds were lined up side by side. Each night I cried into my pillow, not wanting to be like the boys whose cries were loud and nonstop. It was hard to fall asleep with all the crying–theirs and mine. I hid under my thin, scratchy blanket, trying to block out the horrible sounds. I was always a little scared of the watchman walking up and down the aisles with his flashlight. I never saw his face, only his glaring yellow light. I heard his footsteps amongst the boys' cries, sometimes knowing that one of the more distant cries belonged to Coke. Even now, when it's quiet and I'm in bed, I can get kind of leery about nighttime. I worry about someone breaking in, imagining that there's an intruder in the doorway, or some other figure walking about my room like the faceless watchman.

I came to realize that living at Saint Vincent's was something I just had to accept. I didn't want to be there, and I hated that Coke was so sad. He was only seven, and I knew he needed his mom more than I. But there was nothing I could do. I prayed for her to come back and decided I'd just have to make the best of things in the meantime. Sports gave me some welcome distraction from the loneliness and uncertainty about when—or if—our mom would come get us. I put all my energy into doing well on the basketball team. When we won the championship, I was tremendously proud that all my effort had contributed to the big win. We were awarded gold basketball pins, and I wore mine on my green Saint Vincent's Basketball Team sweater every single day.

I made friends with the trouble makers, the Fernandes brothers, who liked breaking the rules. One day they took me out to the long yard in the back of the main building and showed me a tunnel they'd been digging for weeks. It just barely fit the three of us, and we'd sneak in there during recess to smoke the cigarettes they'd somehow gotten their hands on. One day they convinced me to try and run away with them. They told me about a railroad train a mile or two down the road.

"Once we get there, we can leave forever."

"I don't know. It seems kinda risky."

"Come on, Peter. Are you afraid?"

"No," I lied.

And off we went. We got lost in the meadow's tall grass and thickets, not sure which direction would take us closer to the mythical railroad. We were eventually found in the meadows, not far from Saint Vincent's. The sisters were furious. I already thought they were mean–the way they'd make us ball our fists up so they could hit our knuckles with rulers for no reason at all, or how they'd yell at us for talking in class, or the way they'd scold us for not getting ready for school fast enough. But our punishment for running away was the worst. After the predictable scolding and knuckle-hitting, we were told we had to work longer hours in the kitchen. And then we had to stand at attention on the pillar across from the pool for hours on end while the other kids got to swim and play and eat. Some of the kids preferred to stare and point and laugh at us, rather than play in the pool. I couldn't see him, but I knew Coke wasn't laughing. He was probably crying at the sight of his big brother forced to stand there for so long, forced to be humiliated like that. I hoped he hadn't heard any rumors about the reason for our punishment. It would've destroyed him to think that I might have left him there.

I'm not sure what happened to the Fernandes brothers. I heard they were moved to a stricter facility because Saint Vincent's couldn't handle their troublemaking. I wonder if they were able to make something out of their lives or if they stayed stuck in the "bad boy" roles they'd been assigned so long ago.

We had some family visitors now and then. Never my mother though. Sometimes we got visits from my sister Jay and her husband, Vince. We were allowed to leave for a few hours during their visits, but we had to be back by 6 p.m. sharp, no exceptions. They'd take us to Sausalito, where we'd walk along the water. And sometimes we'd get to take the ferry to San Francisco and back. My brother Manuel, the oldest and most responsible sibling, came to visit us a few times as well, when he was on leave from the service. He was almost a father figure in my eyes–tall, mature, hardworking. He and Jay would always tell us that we'd be going home soon. "We'll get you out of here real soon," Manuel would say. "Don't worry," Jay said, wiping Coke's tears from his cheeks. "We'll be taking you out of here real soon." I didn't know what "real soon" meant. Our mom had said that many months ago. "Real soon" felt like an eternity.

One time, when Jay and Vince took us out on the ferry boat, I walked onto the deck by myself and looked out onto the open water. The sunlight twinkled on the surface of the bright blue San Francisco Bay. I took a long deep breath, watching the Sausalito ferry dock fade away as we glided toward the city. I wanted to stop time. But I knew we only had a few more hours. My thoughts drifted back and forth–to my past, and to my future. There had been so many moves, so many changes, and not a lot of the things other kids seemed to have. My family was so broken apart. *I will not keep living like this*, I thought. *I've got to make something out of myself. But how?*

I had no answer to the question of "How?" *How will I change my life for the better? How will I keep things together instead of having everything change and break apart?* One question finally got answered though, the one about when and if I'd ever see my father again. He had remarried by then, and after living in San Antonio, Texas, for a while, he returned to Oakland with his new wife, Cleo. She was a very pretty, slender woman with jet black hair, 16 years younger than my father. When they came to visit us at Saint Vincent's, my father looked happier than I'd ever seen him. His clear skin and bright eyes made me think he must've been slowing down on the drink. Just like my brother and sister, my father assured us we'd be leaving soon. He looked a little upset when he walked to his car. But he seemed a little removed too. With all the drinking he did when we were young, he didn't know us that well. I decided it didn't really matter if he was upset over us being in the boys' home since he was just another family visitor telling us we'd be out of there "real soon." I'd given up hope. It had been almost a year. I figured we were just too expensive for our parents to care for. And, deep down, I figured we must not have been lovable enough. After all, if they'd really loved us, wouldn't they have come for us already?

But one day, a warm one, the sun burning through the Eucalyptus trees lining the courtyard, I saw Jay and Vince pull up. I heard something about payments falling behind. Whoever was paying for Coke and me to be there had stopped. The courts? The government? Some family member? I didn't know. While Coke went running for the car, I stood still. After all that praying and hoping that one day we'd get to leave, here was my chance. But for some reason, a part of me didn't want to leave yet. "Can I stay a few more weeks?" I asked. "The championship game is coming up. We gotta win. My team needs me." The answer was "no." We were told to pack our bags.

By then, the family's whereabouts had shifted some more. After another visit to Mexico, our mom had come back with Alice, leaving Bobby there to continue his schooling. He'd grown very close to our grandparents, so it made the most sense for him to stay. Because of her education and fluency in both English and Spanish, Alice quickly found work in the Oakland school system. The restaurant in Mexico wasn't doing well, so eventually my grandparents decided to sell the business and move back with Bobby to Pittsburgh, California, where they bought a house and retired.

For now, as we learned on the drive from Marin to Oakland, we'd be staying with our dad and Cleo instead of our mother and other siblings. "You're going to Dad's home," Jay said. She didn't give us a reason why, and I didn't want to ask. There was a time when I didn't know if the words "home" and "Dad" would ever go together again. I longed to see my mom, but at the same time I was excited about spending time with him, relishing this feeling that he must've wanted us after all.

Our new home was a small apartment across the street from Saint Francis De Sales church and school.

We tried our best to get used to the new space, but Coke couldn't get along with Cleo. It must have been tough for her to suddenly start raising someone else's kids, especially kids who'd just come out of an orphanage–kids who missed their mom, kids who didn't trust that caregivers would stick around or that a home was a place they were ever really wanted. It was hard for me to shake Saint Vincent's, partly because I wore my green basketball sweater with my gold championship pin every day. I had no choice. It was the only top I had. Day after day, I'd wear it along with the same pair of khaki pants and my only pair of shoes.

CRED

Recently, I had a concert in Napa, California. As we drove along the 101 North toward the venue, I saw the Marinwood exit ahead, the exit that represented one of the most significant changes of direction in my life. I pointed toward the meadows surrounding Saint Vincent's so Juanita could see. "That's where Coke and I stayed as boys," I told her. Her face turned serious. "I want to see it."

I wanted her to see it, but I wasn't sure I could see it again. I decided to face my fear, reminding myself I was in my 70s now, a grown man with my own home and tight family, no longer a little boy without any say about being dropped off in an orphanage. We drove down the road lined with Eucalyptus trees. The speed limit was only 10 miles per hour, so it felt like I had too much time to prepare. Every memory of that first day came back. It was like a recurring nightmare–flashes of familiar terrors and scary images. We approached the office, and instead of being greeted by a cold priest and sisters, we were greeted by a friendly man and woman who told us that the grounds were being remodeled and that most of the building was closed down. I asked if I could look around, telling them that I'd lived there as a young boy. "Was your stay a good one?" asked the woman. "It was an emotional time," was all I could say. I showed

Juanita where the kitchen had been, the place where I stood during punishment, where Coke's room was, and where mine was–where I'd slept in a long line of beds, trying to block the sounds of the boys' cries each night. "Sometimes I heard Coke's cry from across the courtyard," I told Juanita. I saw a tear roll down my wife's cheek. It was time to leave.

CB8O

My stay at Saint Vincent's Home for Boys marked a turning point in my life. It was burned in my memory as a permanent reminder about the importance of family. I promised I would try my best to keep my family together, no matter what. I would love them, guide them, and help them, regardless of who or what they would become.

CHAPTER FOUR

MOVING PICTURES

Eventually Coke and I were sent back to live with our mom, who had moved to a new place by then, a bottom flat over in West Oakland on Linden Street. It had two small bedrooms, a tiny front room, and a kitchen. It was so good to see her, to finally feel the embrace of my mother again. But sometimes I wondered how long it would last. We still visited our father, even though our mother didn't seem to approve. She ragged on him a lot, asking us why we wanted to be around "someone like him." She put him down all the time. "He's no good. He's a drunk." And she seemed jealous of Cleo. "He just wanted a younger wife," she'd say. "Why? I gave him everything." When we talked about him, she couldn't help but smile, but then she'd dog him right after the smile, to cover up the hurt maybe. She never seemed to get over him, despite her angry words. She was 17 when she met him, and he was her first love. She still loved him, even all those years later. And I understood. You couldn't help but love him.

Since our mom couldn't afford to keep us in Catholic School, and since we weren't living in that area anymore, I was enrolled in a new school–Westlake Junior High. Mostly it was made up of Whites and Asians, not a lot of Latin kids. I was shy on my first day, not knowing much about "normal" schools. But I noticed a lot of my old Tomkins Elementary friends were there too, which made things a little easier. I thought about trying out for the basketball team, since I was so good at Saint Vincent's. But I realized that compared to the kids at Westlake, I was way too short. No way was I going to play with all those tall guys.

All my fears about fitting into this new school faded once I made new friends: Bobby Ochoa, Don Kaneshige, Charlie Jenkins, and Bobby Molina. They'd make fun of me for always wearing the same Saint Vincent's basketball sweater and pin. "You must really love that sweater!" they'd tease. "Man, you wear that all the time!" I didn't want to explain that I had no choice.

The guys and I would hang out every day, playing basketball, talking about girls, and listening to music. We were inseparable, and I liked having a little crew. Our own little Rat Pack. Bobby O. was the most popular kid at school. He was a good-looking guy, and all the girls had a crush on him. He lived in West Oakland too, just a few blocks from me. Don lived nearby as well. His family was from Japan, and his dad had a gardening business. His younger brother, John, used to hang out with us as well. Bobby Molina was the quiet one. He loved baseball and would read the *Baseball Sporting Green* every day. He'd also listen to all the games on the radio, keeping box scores, memorizing players' batting averages, and rattling off statistics. And then there was Charlie, the gang leader, who was always up to no good.

Charlie was good at convincing us to join him in his pranks. During recess, he'd encourage us to dump the smaller kids into trash cans for no reason at all. I went along with it and tried to join in with the laughter, but I felt guilty the whole time. On our way home from school one day, Charlie devised a plan: One of us would buy a candy bar while everyone else would stuff whatever we could into our jackets. And when Charlie announced his idea that we all wear leather bomber jackets, that was the end of my green basketball sweater. One day, Charlie showed up at my house in a bright red car that he said his dad let him borrow. We picked up the Kaneshige brothers and both the Bobbys before taking a joy ride all around town. But since Charlie wasn't a great driver, and since his dad had reported the car stolen, we didn't get far. The police took us in, and we were locked up for a couple of hours. Don's brother was crying like a baby, telling us we'd be spending life in prison. I was really worried until Charlie's dad came in and got the charges dropped.

As risky as hanging out with these guys could be, I needed to feel like part of a group. We were poor kids from the other side of town who found each other; having a group of friends was like having a mini-family, a place to belong.

CB⬥EO

Luckily, I had other interests besides following along with the rule-breakers. Singing was becoming my new thing. Bobby Ochoa and I got into the school choir and practiced for hours, determined to get as good as our favorite jazz singer, Billy Eckstine. Prepping for the big assembly, we'd listen to Eckstine's records and try to imitate his smooth style. When the big day came, wearing some cool dress shirts we'd borrowed from Bobby's uncle's closet, we hit the stage and made our big debut. The moment we starting crooning, we were a hit. All the girls loved us. Their attention sparked something in both of us, another compelling reason to try to make our lives about music.

Art was another pastime. I'd always enjoyed drawing. Manuel and Jay liked to sketch, so I got my start in art work just by copying them. I liked losing myself in drawing. It took me somewhere else, away from all the bad stuff I sometimes thought about–sadness about my broken-apart family, worry about money, and fear about the future. I took my first real art class at Westlake Junior High. There was a teacher there–I wish I could remember her name– who was impressed with my drawings. She encouraged me to continue studying art in high school, but I wasn't serious about art. I had music on my mind.

Everyone at Westlake Junior High went to Oakland Tech High because that was the school in their district. I'd expected to go with them but soon found out that, because of where I lived, I'd have to go to McClymonds, a school that was looked down on as a "bad school." Bobby Ochoa had used someone else's address. I was hecka depressed about having to go to another school than him and most of my other friends. I wished I'd thought of giving a fake address. I was really missing the guys–Bobby O., Don, and Bobby M. At least Al Larios would be at McClymonds. He and I cut school a lot. We'd walk from West Oakland all the way up to Oakland Tech to hang out with Don and the two Bobbys at Mosswood Park on West MacArthur.

CR&O

It's funny how some life events, even those you can't find any meaning in at the time, guide you toward who and what you will become. Even though I didn't like my school, I realize now that being there was a turning point for me. Art was the only class I didn't want to cut. It's where I began to define myself, not only as a musician but as an artist as well. Like my last art teacher, the McClymonds art teacher, Mrs. Snee, was very supportive. She told me I could make a living as an artist one day if I wanted to. That seemed too good to be true–making money by simply drawing and painting. She let me use her oil paints in the back of the classroom. I couldn't believe she trusted me with the art supplies she'd never let other students touch. In exchange for making signs announcing school rules and events, I was granted unlimited access to this amazing array of materials and colors. I'd paint back there for hours, making abstracts, murals, some faces, and a lot of trees. Mrs. Snee would occasionally come in and look at my work. She wouldn't say much, mostly offering head nods and encouraging smiles. Occasionally, she'd suggest I consider looking at art as more than just a pastime. "You have a future in art if you want it. Do you want it?"

"Well, I like it," I'd say.

"I can get you into an art college in Oakland after you graduate," she told me. "I'll get you a scholarship." She explained how I could be an apprentice at an advertising company.

All of this was in my future, she assured me, if I wanted it. Soon she let me and my friend Bobby Apodaca, another budding artist, leave the school grounds to draw nearby landscapes. I was used to cutting school, but I couldn't believe my luck that a teacher was actually giving me and my friend permission to leave the campus during school hours.

Despite the art perks provided by Mrs. Snee and the much needed breaks from the humdrum of academics, I struggled to find motivation to show up at school every day. I longed to be with my old friends from Westlake. They'd tell me about all the fun they were having at Oakland Tech while Al and I were stuck in our boring school across town. Eventually the principal called me into his office to discuss my habit of playing hooky. He gave me a serious look. "Peter, what can we do to keep you in school?" I didn't think the answer would please him, but I told him the only truthful thing I could think of.

"Well, if you gave me more art classes, more than just one a day, I'd want to be here more."

To my surprise, I was given four art classes. But I had to promise to stay in school and attend the rest of my classes. I happily agreed and slowly settled into becoming a new kind of student: a good one.

ରେନ୍ତ

And while I was nourishing my love of art, my other love, music, was growing too. I befriended a guy named Otis Green, who'd just moved to town all the way from New York. He taught me that I'd have to look the part before I could truly play the part. Otis dressed sharp every day–a sports coat, shirt, and tie.

"Why do you dress up so much just to come to school?" I asked him.

"I like jazz music," he said. "And I like to dress like my favorite jazz players back in New York."

"Cool. I like jazz music too," I told him. "I want to be a jazz musician one day, I think. A great sax player like Gene Ammons."

"Man," Otis said. "If you want to play sax, then you gotta look like a real sax player. You know, dress hip and look cool."

I decided to heed his advice. I took every cent I had and went down to Edward's on Telegraph in downtown Oakland. I bought a shirt, sports coat, slacks, suit, tie, and some suede shoes. (There was a movie theatre a block up from Edward's. Back then, I had no idea that years later that old movie theatre would be replaced by the Fox Theatre, a concert venue that I'd one day headline.) I proudly wore my new outfit to school every single day. Needless to say, I didn't become that cool sax player. But I never stopped dressing up. I even iron my silk pajamas. I think it's another thing I decided back in the lean years–a commitment I made to myself when I had only one outfit to my name. *When I can afford to dress well, I always will.* Dressing well was something I didn't have access to back then; I simply had no say in the matter. But now that I do, dressing up is a top priority.

As much as I thought about becoming a commercial artist, upon the urging of that wonderful Mrs. Snee who said she'd get me into art college and secure my internship at an advertising company, I couldn't deny my increasing desire to pursue a music career. Al and I would stay up all night listening to records and doing our best to play along. We'd hang out at Bobby's house because he had a piano. We'd jam all night–me on makeshift bongos constructed with coffee cans and tape. Our trio wasn't long-lived because none of us could play that well. So Bobby and I went back to singing. We talked about how great it would be to become professional musicians, to travel and perform all over the world. Al started playing guitar at an early age but had switched over to the bass in high school. I tried out different instruments too. I went from beating on coffee cans, to playing the saxophone, to trying to play vibes. I was the master of none, but I was so eager to play something that I was happy on any instrument.

Al and I soon heard about a great piano player at our school, Ed Kelly. One day we walked up to Ed and asked if he wanted to start a band with us. When Ed said he already had a band with a sax and bass player, we had to think fast.

"How about percussion?" I asked. I did enjoy messing around on the congas and bongos, and I liked the idea of being forced to get good quickly. I'd been listening to some Latin jazz stuff and making frequent trips to our little neighborhood record store to listen to all the big Latin musicians like Tito Puente, Tito Rodriguez, Cachao, Eddie Palmieri, Mongo Santa Maria, Willie Bobo, and Machito.

Ed nodded. "That would be cool. It will help with the Latin songs I want to learn."

And with that, I was a percussionist. Sometimes I wonder how my life would've turned out if Ed didn't already have a sax player. I certainly wouldn't have had the same kind of career. And I might not have had three percussionist children who grew up with more percussion instruments in the house than furniture. We thought Sheila would play violin, Juan would play trumpet, and Peter Michael would play bass, since those are the instruments they started on. But I guess, like their Daddy, they had an undeniable urge to pound on stuff.

⊙⊛⊙

Our band and my Billy Eckstine impersonation began to earn me some popularity points. I wondered, though, if I was good enough to date Carol Prathere. She was the tallest and prettiest girl in school, and she happened to be in our choir. All the boys were after her because she was such a knockout, and since she lived in Piedmont's high-end district, she was considered upper class. Nobody was brave enough to ask her out. But when I found out that she wasn't going with anybody, I thought, "What the heck? Let me give it a try." My plan was to get to know her first. I started talking to her every day, and whenever there were parties or dances, I'd go out of my way to hang out by her. When I finally got the nerve to ask her out on a date to the movies, she said yes. And after a few more dates, I asked her to "go steady."

For us, going steady mostly consisted of meeting at Mosswood Park and sitting on the bench next to the large oak tree where we'd talk for hours–about school, our friends, and our big life dreams. She wanted to teach music, and I wanted to keep making it. Decades later, Carol came up to me after one of my shows at Yoshi's Jazz Club in Oakland, and we hugged and reminisced. She was a music teacher, and I was a working musician. We'd both become what we'd talked about becoming. Dreams do come true. Even those created by kids on a shabby park bench.

CHAPTER FIVE

HAVING A GOOD TIME

Our Ed Kelly Latin jazz band was upping rehearsals and getting better and better by the day. We were beginning to feel like the real deal. We'd meet daily, either at the sax and bass players' house, twin brothers John and Boyd, or at Ed's house in the West Oakland projects.

Ed heard about an amateur contest in Stockton that would be televised on local stations, and we immediately signed up. When we won, our confidence soared. And we won not just once, but every time. Week after week, we were the uncontested winners. We felt unstoppable. When we got to the finals, we just knew we'd win the first prize. (I can't remember what first prize was, but I know we had our hearts set on winning it.) But we lost. And we lost to a girl who twirled a baton. That was a hard one to live down-losing to a baton-twirler.

After that humiliating defeat, we figured we'd lost our chance at fame and fortune. But we were determined to keep playing anyway. So we played wherever we could–at school assemblies, after-school parties, cafés, art galleries, and impromptu jam sessions at restaurants.

Then a new opportunity presented itself, something even more exciting than the Stockton talent contest. A teacher told us about a program allowing high school groups to open for the main act in real nightclubs. Out of all the jazz groups from all the Bay Area public schools, our Ed Kelly Latin Jazz Band was selected to open for a major artist. First we found out about the venue: The Downbeat Club on Market Street in San Francisco. We couldn't believe it. This was a real music club that hosted the best musicians, all the big jazz guys who came through on their tours. And then we found out who we were opening for: The Count Basic Orchestra. At first I thought it was a joke, some kind of prank. But it was for real. And it was this experience–playing at a real club, with excellent musicians, and a paying crowd there to hear good jazz–that would officially convince me that music was my purpose.

The club was buzzing when we got there. We were quickly ushered back stage where I immediately peeked out from the curtain to get a better look. The place was packed full of smartly dressed men and women ready to hear some real live music. I straightened my tie, more nervous than I'd ever been. It felt like all those rehearsals had been for nothing. I couldn't remember what we'd planned to play or how I was supposed to play it. *Will I remember the set? Will I mess up? We're opening up for Count Basie! This ain't no school assembly.*

When they introduced us, the rich sound of applause surprised me. This is what Al and I had been dreaming of. This is what we'd been talking about all those days and nights. I didn't want to mess it up. But we did great, and the crowd loved us. For the first time in my life, I felt like a real musician. And I knew it was the only path I should pursue. I was all in. *This is what I want to be doing from now on*, I thought. *This is what I want my life to be about.*

We didn't get to meet the players in the orchestra because we weren't allowed to be there more than a few minutes before going on stage, and we had to leave right after we played. But I did manage to sneak into an empty hallway in the back corner of the club so I could catch one song. They were smokin'. It was all feeling too good to be true. *They're standing where we just stood. They're playing where we just played. We were on the same stage as the Count Basie Orchestra.*

The father of one of the guys drove us home; he couldn't get us to settle down.

"That was so cool!" Ed exclaimed.

"We gotta keep this up!" I told them.

"Yes!" everybody screamed in unison.

I don't think I slept at all that night. I kept playing the entire event over and over in my mind. I had realized my calling. I had to become a real musician.

CHAPTER SIX

NOW & FOREVER

Juanita Marie Gardere
Born September 8, 1937
Oakland, California

Music continued to be my focus. And even though I didn't know many musicians who made a lot of money, I held onto hope that one day it would get me out of the cramped quarters I'd gotten used to. I was in the eleventh grade, living with my mom on Seventh and Castro in the top apartment facing Old Man's Park. We lived across the street from a worn-down mansion that had once been the mayor's house. It was me, Coke, my mother, and her boyfriend, Steve, a foreman she'd met while working at the cannery. He seemed more like a pool shark than a foreman, wearing fancy-looking suits and going out to the pool hall every night.

The apartment was owned by an Asian family, and we were the only tenants who weren't Asian. The scent of Chinese cooking permeated the building. An army of cockroaches invaded, and it seemed like they lived there while we were just the visitors. Every time I turned on a light, I'd see them scramble. It was another symbol of poverty, of not having control over my living environment. One night, after I flipped on the light switch and saw what seemed like a thousand of them scatter under my cot, again I swore I'd make something out of myself. Music had to give me some kind of way out. Things needed to change.

Those kinds of changes would take a while. But there was another change on the horizon, a big one that I wasn't even looking for. Bobby Ochoa was on the basketball team at Oakland Tech High, and he had befriended his teammate, Harold Gardere. Bobby always used to talk about how friendly and cool Harold and his brothers and sisters were, and how I just had to meet them. One day after school, I finally accepted the invitation and went with him to meet the Garderes.

As we entered the house, they all greeted Bobby with the nickname "Choco." I quickly learned that most of them had nicknames too: Joe was "Kookababy," Curtis was "Lulu," Nick Jr. was "Jr.," Sylvia was "Tut," Evella was "Lala," and Juanita was "Neet." It took me years to learn their real names. The only ones without nicknames were Floyd and Harold.

Nick and Marie Gardere had moved from New Orleans to this big, two-story house at 3303 Market Street in North Oakland. From the looks of this huge house, which wrapped around the street corner, I figured they were rich. Nick Sr., a plasterer, had a large family to take care of, and so he joined his brothers in the family business. He was a strong and hardworking man. Providing for his family was his number one priority. His wife, Marie, was the backbone, caring for her husband and her children with great devotion. Family closeness was something they both valued, so they made sure their children stayed close to each other and close to the nest. Marie made it clear to them that they were not to disturb their father with any childish foolishness. And if they forgot that rule, it only took one stern look from Nick Sr. to refresh their memory.

Nick Sr., who they called "Papa Rock," ran his house like he was a judge presiding over a court. There were a lot of relatives living in this family fortress, and yet it was always clean, organized, and chaos-free. Marie offered a kindness that counteracted her husband's strict nature. They had found a way to strike a nice balance, and I was drawn to the deep family connection I felt the minute I stepped into the house. I couldn't help but compare their family to mine. Mine felt broken–different parts with jagged edges, a bunch of puzzle pieces that never fit together. But here was a family, a solid family, and unlike my broken home, here there was a spirit of connection and permanency I didn't even know I'd been longing for. In their home, I felt a little out of my league. I was just a poor skinny kid from West Oakland, and I could tell Papa Rock didn't know what to make of me.

That first day, I couldn't help but notice pretty Juanita in the corner of the dining room. She was a thin young girl, dressed in a flared skirt, a sweater, shiny white shoes, and bobby socks rolled over her ankles. Like the rest of the family, she had a beautiful light complexion, light eyes, and light hair. She was busily sorting through a pile of 45-records, placing them one by one on the phonograph and singing along. When she looked up, mid-song, our eyes met, and I felt something I'd never felt before.

Choco later told me that Juanita and her siblings looked different because they were Creole, a mixture of French and Black. I'd never heard of a Creole before, so they seemed special and exotic to me. I could tell Juanita had a mad crush on Choco, so I kept my distance. When I cut school, I'd see her at Oakland Tech and over at Dave and Dirk's, where she was always playing pinball. She dominated that pinball machine like her life depended on it. And sometimes I'd see her at the Walgreen's on the corner of 12th and Broadway. Most of the kids would hang inside at the soda fountain, but I preferred to hang outside, where I could watch the girls go by. Whenever Juanita and her friend Margie Hirota passed by, I'd shoot her a smile.

I started calling Juanita and meeting her at her school. I'd walk her home and then take my long walk back from North to West Oakland. Then we'd talk on the phone for hours about everything–our pasts, what we did that day, and what we dreamed about for the future. Soon enough, our individual futures became a shared one. Juanita would serenade me over the phone with songs like *Blue Moon* and *My Funny Valentine*. I could hear her mom in the background telling her it was time to hang up, but we never wanted to say goodbye. Those evening phone calls nourished me. I didn't need to sleep or eat. I just wanted to hear her voice and her laughter. She was the one I wanted to tell everything to.

One night, I invited her to a jam session where Fred Pirtle, a great jazz saxophone player, and Lonnie Hewitt, an excellent piano player, were scheduled to play. Gene Fernandez, a wild kid and a good friend, came along on the date because he had a car. I was used to staying out as late as I wanted, checking out bands, and hanging at jam sessions. I didn't know that Juanita's parents had given her strict orders to be back home by a certain time. So when Gene's car broke down on the way back, and we had to drop Juanita off very late, Nick and Marie were not happy. This was only the first of many nights she wouldn't make curfew. Even when the car was running fine, we found reasons to stay out late. We never wanted to leave each other. So Juanita would often be on punishment, and we could only talk on the phone for limited amounts of time. Sometimes we weren't allowed to see each other for weeks on end. This was big-time punishment for me as well.

♋

Meanwhile, I was still doing my art work, but it was becoming more and more of a pastime. It was music that mattered most. And even with my additional art classes, I began cutting school again. My mom wanted me to stay in school, as did Juanita, but they could both tell I was driven to work, make money, and make music. In terms of school, my heart just wasn't in it. So I made a decision: It was time to leave school for good. I wouldn't graduate or go on to college. I would devote all of my time and energy to a career in music. Was it the right decision? All I had to do was get through a few more months of senior year and accept my art teacher's generous offer to help get me into an art college and an internship. Was I throwing away a chance at a promising creative career so that I could pursue a much less promising one? I knew trying to make it as a professional musician would be an uphill battle. I'd only had a few informal sax lessons and one drum lesson. I knew I could beat on some skins and keep a beat, but I also sensed that I had a whole lot more to learn. Now that I was playing congas and bongos, I had even more to study. I was taking a huge risk, but there was nothing else I felt was worth my blood, sweat, and tears. That night when our Ed Kelly Jazz band had opened for Count Basie, I'd discovered that music was my calling. And I was ready to heed the call.

So when I wasn't spending time with Juanita, I was looking for legitimate work as a musician. I met a pianist and composer from Panama, Carlos Federico, who invited me to check him out at the California Hotel Gold Room's Sunday Mambo Sessions. I couldn't wait to see him play live. I'd already seen him perform on a TV show, *Sepia Review*, hosted by former Oakland Bittners basketball player, Don Barksdale. Carlos had some great percussion players in his band–Ricardo Lewis on congas, Benny Velarde on timbales, and Carlos Bruins on hand percussion. (And he had a bunch of great bass players and vibe players over the years.) I started going every Sunday. Some friends from back east had recently taught me all the cool dance steps, and I loved hitting the floor and showing off my moves. At the time, Willy Vargas was the timbale player. When I heard he was leaving the band because he got a gig in Las Vegas, I knew this could be a great opportunity for me to join a real band. So the next Sunday night, I mustered up the nerve to ask Carlos if I could audition. "Sure," he said. "Come to my house next week."

I'd memorized every song the band played, having been to all the Sunday night shows for weeks. So when I arrived, I felt pretty confident. As I started playing, Carlos and the other band members looked at me with amazement. I knew every break and tempo, as well as each song's name. I even knew the originals that Carlos had written, like *Jose* and *Bartok*. "You're hired, man," Carlos said. "Can you start next Sunday?

I tried to play it cool. "Yeah, I think so," I told him.

"Let me just check my calendar first."

"Great," Carlos said. "If you can start then, be sure to wear a black suit and a red tie. And, of course, make sure you're in the union."

Black suit? No problem. Red tie? Sure. But union? What the heck is a union?

The very next morning, I asked around and finally got directed to the Musicians Union Local 6. I scheduled an appointment and was issued my very first union card. Now it was official. I was a working musician. Once I paid the initiation fee and the work dues, I could play anywhere. My career was beginning.

Since I still didn't have my own car, I had to catch the bus by my apartment. I carried my timbales in a flour sack on one arm and the cymbal on the other. (These timbales were a gift from my friend Al. More on that later.) After the gig, I'd find someone to give me a lift home. I loved this steady, weekly gig. We had a regular crowd every Sunday, so it was like being part of a new community. I knew I had a lot to learn as a musician, and I took it seriously. It was like going to school all over again, only this time I cared about each and every lesson. I was the youngest one in the band, so I did a lot of listening. I paid close attention not just to what they played but also how they played. I watched how the guys carried themselves too.

The rest of the week, I still had my daily routine of getting dressed up, walking to town, and hanging out in front of Walgreen's, just people-watching, and hoping I looked cool to any people who might be watching me back. Once I turned the corner of our block on my way back home, I'd hear Coke playing my timbales. Even though I was annoyed that he'd taken them out, I was impressed by how good he was sounding. He was getting better than me.

When I found out one of the guys in Carlos' band was leaving, I told him about Coke. "Man, my brother plays better than I do," I said. "He could take over the timbales, and I'll switch to congas. He knows all the songs too." And with my enthusiastic endorsement, Coke was in. After that, lots of different bands started hiring us together as a kind of duo.

 beckett

The other duo–Juanita and I–was getting stronger by the day. And our inability to stay apart was still getting us into trouble. One day, I convinced Juanita to skip school and come over to my place. My mom was supposed to be at work, but when we heard her come home early, Juanita had to run to the closet and hide. Mom discovered her–must have been the high-pitched giggles that gave her away–and Mom was not pleased. She called Nick Sr. and Marie, and they immediately came over to pick Juanita up and put her on yet another punishment. I guess that's love. We were willing to risk a whole lot of punishment just to be together. I had experienced an undeniable draw to music, and now I was experiencing an undeniable draw to a young woman. Music and Juanita had both taken hold of me, and that was just fine by me.

CHAPTER SEVEN
NINA

I believe that despite all my intentions and strategies, God is the only one with any kind of master plan. I knew Juanita was the one for me. And I knew that music was the only career worth pursuing. But I didn't know how my love for both would define my life or the lives of my future children. I was certain that Juanita loved me back, but with music, I had less confidence. And I had no idea how—or if—I'd get to express myself through music in any kind of meaningful way. With hindsight, I can see how one part of God's larger plan presented itself in the form of a birthday present.

Al Larios showed up at my apartment with some timbales in hand. Without saying more than "Happy Birthday," he began setting them up–twisting the cymbals on and adjusting the stands. I was confused. "Why are these timbales here?"

"This is your birthday present. Learn how to play them."

And so I did. I had just turned 18, and I had been given a gift that would last a lifetime.

Those were the timbales I'd lug around in a flour sack because I was without a car for years. When I needed a break from timbale practice, I'd go for my usual walk–strolling along Old Man's Park, cutting through Hales department store, and ending up at Walgreen's. Sometimes I bought dress clothes at a spot up the street–always on layaway. I only had a little money saved up from working at the cannery during summertime, and my only steady source of income was those weekly gigs with Carlos. It always took me a long time to pay off my balance.

My mom was starting to get on my case about finding a real job. "Forget about the music business," she'd say. "You need something reliable."

"But it's what I really want to do," I explained.

Even when she bugged me about finding a "real job," I think she knew I'd never give up my dream. One day, while out for my regular walk towards downtown, I neared the end of the block and heard some music coming from the upstairs of the corner apartment. I noticed a guy sitting on the front steps.

"Hey, do you know who's playing that music?" I asked him.

"It's some guy who lives here. He's always blasting music on his phonograph."

I later learned that this guy's name was Joe Ross, and he'd recently moved to Oakland from New York along with his brother, Ernie, and his sister, Eva. He and his brother were both musicians, and they knew all the hippest dance steps from back east. They also had a small band with their uncle, Willy Vargas, and they played every Saturday night at the Keystone Hall on Franklin Street. Joe turned me on to all the great Latin music from Cuba, Puerto Rico, and New York. Sometimes Al Larios and I would sit in with their band. The four of us would jam, listen to Latin jazz, and fantasize about how life would be if we could just make it in show business.

෬෨

After Juanita graduated high school, she went to work in an office as a bookkeeper. Sometimes she'd babysit her sister Evella's kids, Anna Marie and Bobby (a.k.a. "Big Shot"). They lived in a converted garage behind the main house. I'd sneak over there at night whenever I could. One night, when Evella returned much earlier than expected, I ran upstairs and climbed out the window onto the roof. I had to wait in the cold for everyone to go to sleep before I could make my escape. I was shivering up there for hours.

Clearly, Juanita and I just couldn't stay away from each other for long. We'd begun talking about "forever," and the word "marriage" came up a lot. Juanita told me that I'd have to ask her father for permission. I was terrified. Papa Rock did not think of me as an ideal son-in-law; this I knew. I was a starving musician with no reliable day job. Plus, in those days, interracial marriages weren't exactly embraced. He and Marie wanted Juanita to end up with an upstanding Creole, not a Mexican musician from the hood. Kids were to marry within their race. My parents were pretty old-school too. They didn't want me ending up with a Creole (which at the time was the same thing as "Negro") any more than her parents wanted their daughter with a Mexican.

Despite our parents' concern about race, Juanita and I didn't pay much attention to racial issues. Within Juanita's Creole family, lighter skin was better, as it was associated with a higher class. One of her uncles was a lot darker than the other relatives, and he was treated poorly because of it. Juanita didn't like witnessing that kind of prejudice, so from a very young age, she made it a point to treat all people equally. Growing up in the very ethnically and culturally diverse Oakland neighborhoods, I came across people of all colors and backgrounds and didn't have any preconceived notions about race. I lived in mostly black neighborhoods. When people looked down on me, I assumed it was because I was poor, not because of the color of my skin. I just wasn't trippin' on the race thing. I had friends who were White, Black, Creole, Mexican, and Asian. And we all got along well.

During junior high, I grew more aware of the racial and class divides. Most of us Latin guys lived in West Oakland, and all the white kids seemed to live above MacArthur Boulevard in Piedmont. One time, even though we weren't invited, we went to a party in Piedmont. When we got there, they looked at us funny. "You don't belong here," one of the white boys said to us. We didn't stay long. I was confused. "They think we're lower class because we're Latin," one of the boys explained on our way home. But that was really the worst of it. For the most part, maybe because I was fortunate enough to grow up in the liberal San Francisco Bay Area, I didn't witness too much obvious racism.

But Juanita's father was from a different place and time. So getting up the nerve to ask for his daughter's hand in marriage took me a while. I was familiar with his daily routine: When he came home from work, he'd go outside to water the lawn. That's where I planned to meet him, but it took me weeks to build up the courage. One day, when he came out to the lawn, there I was, waiting for him. I hoped he didn't notice my hands trembling. He stared at me, waiting for me to speak. I blurted it out. "I want to ask your daughter to marry me," I stammered. "I hope you'll give me your blessing." He looked at me like I was crazy. "Why are you asking now? I know you already plan to do it anyway." I took that as the best "yes" I could get. I ran upstairs to where Juanita and her mother were waiting. "I guess he said it was okay," I told them. Marie laughed and Juanita gave me a big hug.

Over time, our parents couldn't deny how happy we made each other, and eventually they gave us their blessings. We married on October 21, 1956, at Saint Andrews Church on Adeline Street in North Oakland. My best man was Al Larios and my groomsmen were my brother Manuel, Fred Lara, and Richard Arriola. Juanita's sister Sylvia was her maid of honor and her bridesmaids were my sister Jay Gardere, Pat Bell, Doris Gardere, and Dolores Dimelo. My father was the only one missing. Sadly, I was used to that. The reception at Eagles Hall in Piedmont was filled with relatives, friends, and musicians. It was a huge party. At the end of the night, we all ended up at the California Hotel Gold Room, where we continued the celebration at Carlos' Mambo Sessions. It was perfect.

CHAPTER EIGHT

UN POQUITO

Juanita and I settled into a small apartment for $50 a month on Adeline Street on the Berkeley/Oakland border. We liked to say that our backyard was in Berkeley and our front yard was in Oakland. It was the lower flat of a two-story building behind the owner's house. Our upstairs neighbors were Mr. Dixon, who owned a Texaco gas station on the other side of town over by Seventh Street in West Oakland, and his daughter, Layla. Since Juanita and I wanted to start a family right away, dreaming of having six children, I had to get a day job. Juanita worked at Borden's Ice Cream Factory, and I still had just the one gig with Carlos. We needed more.

Mr. Dixon was kind enough to let me work at his gas station. I felt pretty goofy wearing the uniform–khaki pants, a khaki shirt with a big Texaco star on the back, and a plastic bow tie. I had to say my lines each time a customer came up. "Hi there. Fill it up with Texaco?" I didn't know how to open the hood, and I could never find the dip stick to check the oil. I have to admit, I was a terrible gas station attendant.

One time, a customer came in with a flat tire. I fixed it to the best of my ability, proud of myself for managing this job without any formal training. The customer drove off looking satisfied but came back yelling at me 20 minutes later. "I almost got in an accident," she screamed. "The tire came off!" I guess I'd forgotten to tighten the bolts. And that, needless to say, was my last day on the job. I never felt cut out to be a 9-to-5 worker. My summer jobs at Del Monte Cannery were pretty bad because I wasn't fast or focused. And after two days at the glass company where my brother Manuel worked, I got fired because I broke just about every glass pane I put my hands on.

Soon enough, despite our financial strain, we found out that Juanita was pregnant with our first child, and we were ecstatic. If it was a boy, we'd likely name him Peter Jr., but if it was a girl, we had no idea. We just couldn't seem to settle on a name. Layla, our upstairs neighbor, suggested the first name Sheila and the middle name Cecilia, after Saint Cecilia, the Patron Saint of Musicians. We liked the sound of that. And on December 12, 1957, our Sheila Cecilia Escovedo was born.

It was still hard for me to earn a consistent living as a musician. So as soon as Juanita could go back to work, I became the stay-at-home Dad, taking care of Sheila as best I could. Whenever I had daytime rehearsals or gigs, I'd take her along with me. And since Juanita often worked the late shift, I'd bring Sheila to the club gigs too. She really was born into music, sleeping in her bassinet on the side of the stage or in club booths as waitresses cooed over her. When bands or club owners complained, I told them I had no other option. We were a package deal.

Early on, it was clear that Sheila was drawn to music. Whenever this one Jiffy peanut butter commercial came on, she'd quickly crawl over to the TV–all smiles and laughter– and pat her hands along to the music jingle which had a heavy drum beat. Her timing was perfection. I think it was this jingle that made her learn to crawl so quickly. She wanted to get as close to the source of that beat and catchy melody as she possibly could. As soon as she could reach my conga drums, which I kept in the front room of our apartment, I couldn't keep her little hands off them. She liked to sit across from me and copy my hands while I practiced to my record collection. She was my little mirror image. Whatever my right hand would do, her left hand would do. Whatever my left hand would do, her right hand would do. That's why, to this day, she plays "backwards"–all from sitting across from me and mirroring my movements. I had no idea she'd become a drummer one day, but it's almost like she had no choice.

I was delighted when she took up the violin in grammar school. I knew she had exceptional musical talent, and I was hoping she'd take to a classical instrument. It would open up so many more possibilities for her. I envisioned her scoring music for symphonies. Better that than being on the same path as me–struggling financially with very few options.

One day I got a call from Sheila's music teacher. "You know, you have a really talented daughter. She's way ahead of the class. And she learns everything right away."

"That's great," I said.

"The problem is, she's not reading the music. She's pretending to."

"What? She's not reading?"

"Well, she doesn't need to. She hears it once and then memorizes it. Then she plays it back right away. Perfectly."

Despite her talent as a violinist and the many scholarship offers she got, Sheila had her heart set on percussion. She was being teased for playing the "square" violin, and she much preferred her Daddy's instruments.

CHAPTER NINE

BOOMERANG

Our financial problems were getting worse, so my friend Richard Arriola moved in to help with the rent. Since my gigs weren't paying that well, Juanita had to keep working. And just a few days after we discovered we were expecting another child, our landlord told us he was raising our rent from $55 to $65 a month. This extra $10 would be too much. So we moved into the small house in Juanita's parents' backyard. It was a garage that Papa Rock had turned into a mini-apartment. In wintertime, there was mildew on the walls. This was a low point.

But the blessing of that year was the birth of our second child, my first son, Juan José Escovedo, born March 13, 1959. I still can't really remember why we named him Juan. I did have a friend from Mexico named Juan who used to hang out with me a lot back then. Maybe that's where we got the name. Or maybe it was because we liked that it was the first part of Juanita's name. Juan likes to tease us about our nonchalance. "You guys can't even remember why you chose my name? What's up with *that*?" Sheila will then chime in. "Well, they got my name because a neighbor they barely knew suggested it. What's up with that?"

A few months after Juan was born, we'd saved up enough money to move to another apartment. It was small, but definitely a step up from that makeshift garage. I was really hustling to get more work. There was an extra mouth to feed, and I wanted to feel like more of a provider. I didn't want my family to have to keep relying on Blue Chip food stamps. I was at the Sands Ballroom in Oakland every Sunday. It was a cool spot where a lot of out-of-town Latin bands performed. I'd dance, soak in the sounds, and hope to somehow get some work. One night, I was especially excited to see this one band from Los Angeles, the Rene Touzet Orchestra, since I'd been listening to their records a lot. I knew a few musicians in the band, and they asked me to sit in and sing a song with them. I sang *La Noche de Anoche*, one of Rene's ballads. I guess I did a pretty good job because a few weeks later he called and asked if I wanted to go to Palm Springs with his band. I couldn't believe I was being asked to play outside of the Bay Area. This is what I'd been looking for–the chance to play on the road with an established orchestra. I couldn't wait. But first I had to figure out the logistics since Rene didn't cover travel and lodging expenses.

I asked Al Larios if he'd come down to Palm Springs with me and help me get situated. This was new territory for me, in more ways than one, and I wanted a little support. "I'm in," he told me. We were ready for the adventure. We'd load my car with luggage and conga drums, drive it there, and then Al would catch the bus home.

Since this job came up, Juanita, the kids, and I were able to move to a nicer place in a better neighborhood. We took the little furniture we had and moved into our new apartment on Sycamore Street. Once we were settled, Al and I were ready to hit the road for Palm Springs. When we got there, we first checked out the Riviera Hotel. It was way too expensive for me, but we enjoyed walking around and entertaining the fantasy of staying there. After driving around town for a few hours, we found a small studio apartment at the end of a motel lot. It was affordable, $50 per week, and close enough to the gig. The landlady told me a lot of entertainers stayed there, and that pretty much sealed the deal. The best part was that I had access to the pool. Al stayed for a night and then headed back to Oakland the next morning. I loved my new nightly gig. There were always big crowds of music lovers and great dancers. I got close to the timbale player, the bass player, and the trumpet player, and we'd hang out after each show, shooting the breeze over a few drinks, and talking about–what else?–music.

The trumpet player soon hooked up with an art student who lived in the desert. When she found out I painted, she invited me over to see her studio. It was a serene space with a gorgeous view, and she was generous enough to let me paint there whenever I wanted. Being out on the road like this was brand new to me, and I was feeling a bit lonely and homesick. (This was, of course, pre-cell phone, and I couldn't even afford a regular landline. So, I'd just write letters to Juanita and anxiously await her reply.) Painting in this studio was a great way to pass the time and distract myself from how much I missed my wife and kids. I painted a few abstracts full of bright reds and oranges inspired by the sun-blasted desert outside her windows. I also made a painting of her and gave it to her as a thank-you gift.

The thought of spending Christmas alone in Palm Springs was unbearable, so I arranged for Juanita, Sheila, and Juan to join me for a few weeks. They took a long bus ride to Palm Springs, and we were reunited for the holidays. We got a few gifts for the kids, a small tree, and some ornaments. It wasn't a typical holiday, but we were together again as a family, and I couldn't have been happier. Each day, we took Sheila and Juan to the nearby playground and the hotel pool. Their visit went way too fast. When it was time for them to head back to Oakland, my chest felt tight. As I watched the bus leave, I waved goodbye and forced a smile. My heart hurt.

I lasted two more months out in Palm Springs. That was all I could take. I said my goodbyes to the band and headed back to Oakland. I hadn't spent a lot of time at our new apartment on Sycamore Street because I'd left for Palm Springs right after we'd moved in. But I'd only get a few more days in this apartment because we got notice from the landlord that we had to be out in two weeks. A few days before I returned, Juanita had thrown a birthday party for our sister-in-law Pee-wee. The party got out of hand–a big fight, windows smashed, and furniture thrown. Our neighbors weren't happy. And when the landlord heard about it, we were out.

Usually we had to move because we couldn't afford rent. This was the first time we had to move because we'd been disruptive. We were used to moving though. It's just the way it was for a long time. We found another place nearby, a second-floor apartment run by a dear older woman named Mary, who let us move in right away. Soon we were expecting our third child, conceived in Palm Springs. On July 7, 1960, Peter Michael Escovedo was born. It's strange that we didn't name our first-born son, Juan, after me. But my father, Peter Michael, named his first-born son Manuel. And I was the second-born son, named after my father. So I kept with this unusual sequence.

CHAPTER TEN

LIKE A VOLCANO

Since Juanita had three young kids to take care of, she couldn't work outside the home anymore. I was feeling the pressure to make more money for my growing family. I joined a small group Coke had been playing with, The Duran Brothers. Manny and Carlos were Cal Tjader's original piano and bass players. We got lots of work around the Bay Area and started to develop a pretty good following. It was great to be gigging so often.

The music scene was all about late nights and lots of hanging. Sure, we worked hard at rehearsals and gigs, but when the show ended, the partying began. And gradually, this partying led me to a stage of my life that I'm deeply ashamed of. I understand how easy it is to give in to temptation, to lose your way, and to find yourself living in a dark underworld. I understand because it happened to me.

It started with drinking too much. I enjoyed having a few drinks with the fellas, but soon a few drinks became too many. And then I started to experiment with drugs. Why in the world did I travel down this road? I have no reasonable excuse. I'd been witness to the kind of destruction alcoholism can cause. I saw how liquor turned my father into a different person, how this different person broke my mother's heart, and how his desire to be intoxicated broke up our family. But for some reason, I too would take a turn down this path, a path that would cost me and my family a lot.

The drug use started because, as cliché as it sounds, it's what everyone around me was doing. It seemed harmless at first. I thought it was cool to be high, that it gave me an extra boost of confidence on stage and it guaranteed me the kind of good time I couldn't have sober. But the good times at the beginning of the night soon led to some bad times at the end of the night.

One night, I drove home in a pretty messed up state, parked my Chevy, and stumbled into the house. Just as I was getting ready to fall into bed, I heard a loud knocking on our door. I opened it to find two serious-looking police officers staring me down.

"Do you own a green 1954 Chevy?"

"Uh, yeah. I do."

"Where'd you park it?

I pointed. "Over there. Across the street." I stepped out and squinted my eyes, trying to find the space on the street where I'd just parked my car. "Wait, it's not there anymore. Somebody stole my car!"

"No," said one of the officers. "It rolled down the hill, flew through two intersections, and then crashed through the window of the corner store."

"Are you serious?" I thought back to my drive home and to parking my car. That's when it hit me: I hadn't put the brakes on or curbed the wheel.

Thank God nobody was hurt. I could've caused an accident driving home. My car could've hit pedestrians when it was cascading down the hill. The police figured I'd just been forgetful, and they didn't question me further. The owners of the store were furious though. "Look what your car did," they screamed at me as I walked around their store to assess the damage. The car was ruined, of course. It had hit the curb, bounced up high, and then crashed through their store. I thought for sure they'd sue me, and I'd be off to jail. But somehow I didn't get into any trouble. As I tried to fall asleep that night, I punished myself with my thoughts. I just kept staring at the ceiling, replaying the events of the night, so angry at myself, and so embarrassed. All of that damage I caused just because I was high. After trying my best to explain my dangerous mistake to Juanita, she and I spent some time praying, thanking God nobody was hurt. Always one to find the silver lining, my sweet wife tried to reassure me. "It could've been so much worse." I nodded in agreement, hoping the morning would bring some peace, some sense of a clean slate.

You'd think that car incident was a wake-up call. But it wasn't. All I really learned from that night was to be sure to set my brakes. I was still living in a culture that supported getting high. It was the times, it was the Bay Area, it was the music scene, and it was just what people around me were doing. *Let's smoke a joint. Let's get a drink. Let's snort some coke.* Drugs and booze were right out there in the open. Lots of guys actually wore a vile filled with cocaine around their necks. That drug was everywhere I went–the streets of Oakland, Berkeley, San Francisco, every bar, and every club. Guys would put lines of coke on the bar in front of everyone. Doctors and lawyers were doing it. I don't think many people realized yet just how dangerous and addictive it was. Musicians seemed to think it helped them play better. It did help us stay up late, but I don't think it made anybody sound better. We just thought we did. And when we woke up the next morning, we couldn't even remember what we played.

Juanita had no idea I was doing cocaine. When she first caught me smoking weed, she was furious. "Why are you doing that stuff?" she asked. She had been raised in such a strict, structured, and family-oriented home. She was always so innocent. So there was no way I was going to let her know I was doing this harder drug. When I didn't come home until the next morning, I told her it was because we played late, hiding the fact that I'd really just been up all night partying.

I continued down this spiral of booze and drugs until I had what felt like a nervous breakdown. I was at some little gig in Modesto, playing with Carlos Federico. Coke was still in the band too. Before we went on, one of the guys handed me a little square of paper and said, "Take this. You'll see stuff you've never seen before."

"What's it called?"

"Acid."

I'd heard of acid, but I didn't know much about it. I figured it would just be another kind of high, so I put it on my tongue like they told me to and waited to see what would happen. I don't remember anything about the gig that night. Everybody told me I walked out into the audience, danced, and acted crazy. When I got back to the hotel, I started hallucinating. I caught a glimpse of my reflection in the mirror. My face was shrinking and soon became the face of a skeleton. I couldn't breathe. Somebody later told me the worst thing to do on LSD is to look in the mirror. But I never got that warning. My panic attack was getting so bad that I called Coke, who was staying in the room down the hall. "You're just having a bad trip," he told me.

But the panic symptoms wouldn't stop. My heart felt like it was jumping out of my chest. That image of my face in the mirror—a shrunken skeleton—wouldn't leave my head. Coke ended up calling the ambulance, and they took me to the hospital. They asked me what I took, and I told them. They gave me something to help me calm down, and I slept for hours. When I woke up, I didn't feel high anymore, but I wasn't myself. I was scared and humiliated.

I couldn't play gigs for a long time after that. I'd get a few words of a song out and then walk off stage. One night, I was playing at a place called Virginia's in Los Angeles, and after just one song, I had to walk off the bandstand because I couldn't find my breath. I cried a lot. I had more panic attacks. I was a mess for about a year–afraid of everything, depressed, and agoraphobic. I took tranquilizers to calm down. I woke up sweating from nightmares. I got very thin because I lost my appetite. I did my best to hide my fear and depression from my wife and kids, telling them I was sick and had to lie down, afraid they'd worry about me if I told them the truth. I did some painting but kept turning down gigs. Coke, the only one who really knew what happened, was getting more and more concerned. "You gotta get it together, man," he'd say. "You gotta get back to your old self."

I needed to snap out of it. I started to take short walks around Lake Merritt, and then I began to run. I'd tell myself, "It'd be cool if you could run around this whole lake." I set small goals–to that tree, to that telephone post, to that garbage can. I got faster and faster, stronger and stronger, and soon I was running the entire lake. Then I set the goal of running around the lake twice. My body and spirit were getting stronger, so I started running local races and then committed to running a marathon.

Running changed my life. I was feeling healthier than ever, and my confidence was renewed. Finally, I was ready to play again. I suppose that if I hadn't gone through that terrible time, I might have gone on to harder drugs, or ended up on the bad side permanently. By crawling out of my hole and seeking solace in running, I became a stronger person with an unshakable respect for the human body.

We all make mistakes in life, and God knows I've made plenty. But it's what we do with what we learn from those mistakes that matters. I'm grateful that I was able to change. I believe we all have the power to change. And it's a blessing that, with God's grace, I changed when I did. Once I let go of all that partying, I could refocus and truly honor the gift of music. I could also be present to my wife and kids in a new way. Without the lessons learned from this dark descent, I may not have discovered such profound gratitude for my family.

CHAPTER ELEVEN
STILL LIFE

Meanwhile, I wasn't the only one who'd been growing a family. My brother Manuel married Virginia, my sister Jay married Virginia's brother Vince, my brother Bobby married Annie, and my sister Alice married Tommy. Soon after moving in with Alice and Tommy, Coke married Norma. And everyone was having babies.

Since my grandparents had moved back to Pittsburg from Mexico, Jamos had become sick with cancer. His decline was gradual, and it was hard to watch him get weaker and weaker. Eventually, he lost the battle and passed away. Abuelita, suddenly alone after so many years of marriage, moved to Oakland to stay downstairs in a lower flat on 13th Avenue, beneath Bobby and Annie. One morning she was on the back porch hanging clothes on the line when she lost her balance and fell far to the ground below. No one knows how long she was lying there before Annie returned to find her. She was rushed to the hospital, where doctors said she was in critical condition. She had severe internal bleeding, and she didn't survive. I was deeply saddened by the loss. I couldn't shake the thought that she had died of being alone.

03❧80

Eventually, Juanita, the kids, and I ended up moving into that same bottom flat. Most of our friends couldn't afford to go out to clubs, so our home became the club–a club with no cover and no closing time. Anytime one of the Latin bands, like Eddie Palmieri's, came to town, they'd end up making our home the location of the after-party. It was just like my parents' house back in those early days–full of music, dance, and drinking. Sheila, Juan, and Peter Michael heard Latin rhythms instead of bedtime lullabies and tales from the road instead of bedtime stories. They were a lot like me and Coke as little kids, wanting to be close to the music and doing anything they could to learn more about it. The difference was, Coke and I would mostly go out and study live music as well as listen to records. My kids learned from being smack-dab in the middle of my rehearsals and jam sessions in the front room. Juanita and I didn't exactly run a structured home where the kids had to do homework and be in bed at a certain time. They were right there in the mix– playing percussion in their pajamas, trying to be part of the party, and soaking in the rhythms and sounds that would eventually inspire them to become musicians themselves.

Tito Puente was another one of the regular fixtures in our front room. I was 18 when I first met him. He was playing his first ever San Francisco gig at Club Macumba on Grant Street in Chinatown. It was a spot that featured Latin music seven nights a week. Cal Tjader was the first to perform there, followed by Joe Loco, Tito Rodrigues, Manny Lopez, and then Tito Puente. It was a great time of befriending all these amazing players, the ones whose records I'd play over and over, like Mongo Santamaria, Willie Bobo, Cal Tjader, and the one who'd become one of my very closest friends, Tito. Back then, Coke and I were just anxious to play, and so we were there every night, taking advantage of any opportunity to see these great live bands do their thing. Just like our dad, we made it a point to hang out with the musicians–before the show, after the show, and between sets. And also just like our dad, we'd invite them over to our house for dinner and drinks and late night talks about our favorite subject in all the world: music. We asked a million questions. "How do you do this? How do you play that? What kind of rhythm is this? What do you call that?" Everybody wanted to learn from them, but you couldn't buy a lesson. And there was this unwritten rule that if you weren't Cuban or Puerto Rican, you had no business playing those instruments. So to become their friends and learn from them, to be taken under their wings like that–what a blessing! Hanging with those guys, that was our school. Real life master classes every night.

The Bay Area seemed to be buzzing with talent and music, and a lot of the guys were either from the Bay Area or ended up settling there. This was, of course, great news for us because it meant we got to hang and play with them more and more. Benny Velarde, Chico Ochoa, and The Duran Brothers were living in the Bay. Armando Peraza was playing with George Shearing and then ended up staying in San Francisco. And when Mongo Santamaria and Willie Bobo left Tito, they joined Cal Tjader's band; so they lived in San Francisco too.

My friendship with Tito would become the strongest of them all. It was a friendship that would last until his death. It's still lasting, really. I often feel his influence and his spirit. Juanita and the kids got close to Tito too. Little Sheila began to call him Uncle Tito, but he insisted on Godfather Tito. As the kids grew older, whenever Sheila and the boys and I played in New York, he'd join us on stage. It was the best of times.

Back then, while the laughter, the number of house guests, and the music was overflowing, my pockets still were not. I couldn't always make rent at the 13th Avenue home, so it was time for the Escovedo family to change addresses once again. Coke and I were still working around town and doing okay financially, but we wanted to be doing better than just okay. I found a house for rent on 16th Street and 21st Avenue in Oakland. It was pretty run down, so I did a little remodeling and gave the inside a fresh coat of paint. We also bought some new furniture with the extra cash I'd saved up. Tito and his band were in town for the housewarming party.

During the daytime, I worked on my paintings. I spent hours playing with color and exploring shapes and faces. During those long periods of time in front of the canvas, I felt like I was searching for something. For what, I didn't know. Even though I was gigging a lot, I still worried about money, and I felt unclear about where I was going in the music business.

When we fell on hard times again, we invited Juanita's brother Joe ("Kookababy") to move in, which helped with the rent. We were doing okay again for a while, until the landlord found out that Juan and Peter Michael had accidentally burned down the garage while playing with matches. That's when we came home to a surprise on our front door: another 30 days' notice.

Thankfully, there were some better surprises around the bend.

CHAPTER TWELVE

LA FAMILIA

As kids, Coke and I were used to unanswered questions about our family. When we were in our 20s, we found out there was even more family-tree mystery than we ever could've imagined. One night, we were gigging at a little Italian restaurant in San Francisco on Grant Street. It was kind of strange to play at a restaurant while folks slurped up their pasta, but the owner liked having live music on weekends, and we were taking whatever work we could find. We worked for tips, usually splitting $25 to $50 between each band member. There was no set band at that point; we just brought along whichever guys were available that night. I'd play congas, Coke would play timbales, and we'd try to get a horn player, a guitar player, a bass player, and a piano player. Eventually we'd bring in trumpets, but we weren't there yet.

Between sets one night, a young bassist struck up a conversation with me and Coke. A few minutes into the conversation, as casually as he'd told us his first name, Phil, he said something that made my jaw drop: "You know what, I think we're related." I took a moment to replay his words in my mind. There was dead silence before Coke jumped in. "Say what?"

"My last name's Escovedo," he explained. "But none of my brothers and sisters have my last name." He paused. "I mean, *our* last name." Since we weren't saying anything, he kept talking. "When I was a teenager, I started asking my mother why I was an Escovedo and nobody else was."

I still didn't know what to say. "What?" was all I could get out.

Coke leaned in. *"Our* dad is *your* dad?"

"Yeah. I didn't know about you guys or his other family until I got into music. Then I started thinking, 'How common is our last name?'"

"So you're our younger brother?" I asked.

"I think so."

Coke and I asked our mom about it the next day. She quickly changed the subject, but she must have known. It's like she knew, without knowing, that her supposed best friend had had some kind of relationship or at least a one-time encounter with our dad. Our sister Jay didn't want to say too much when we grilled her about it. But Jay didn't deny it either. "It's probably true," was all she said.

Even though it was weird for Coke and me at first, we thought about how tough it must have been on Phil all those years. We liked him, and he was a good bass player. He was part of our family, so why not make him part of our band? And thus, we became The Escovedo Brothers. We played in jazz clubs around the Bay Area and eventually expanded into a sextet, playing all the dance halls and steadily gaining a lot of popularity. We used lots of different guys, all really talented, like pianist Don Jordan from back east, Mel Martin on saxophone, and Al Bent on trombone. With our larger band, when we were doing the Latin dance thing, we had Carlos Federico on piano, James Levi on drums, and four trumpet players. Sometimes we had Willie Colon on percussion. We played everywhere–The Jazz Workshop, the Matador, Basin Street West. We opened a lot of places and closed a lot of places. We got to be pretty popular in California as a Latin jazz combo group since not a lot of guys were doing it as frequently and as visibly as we were.

While suddenly having a new brother was pretty strange, Coke and I were able to adjust to the news pretty quickly because family had never seemed like a steady, certain, or wholly know-able thing. A new brother was just one of many unexpected things having to do with our family–a family full of secrets, unexplained mysteries, and incomplete narratives. Years later, Phil got to know our dad, who eventually accepted him and loved him as his son, though I'm sure it was impossible to make up for lost time.

We learned about my father's second family, his family from Texas, only after they'd moved to Huntington Beach. We visited them whenever we played in Los Angeles. It was great getting to know our new siblings. We liked that they thought Coke and I were big stars. The girls are Dolly (Esmerelda, but nobody liked calling her that) and Adelecia ("Cookie"). The three boys became wonderful musicians/guitarists: Alejandro, Javier, and Mario. Funny how Dad's boys from one family took up percussion, while his boys from the other took up guitar.

It was great to get to know our other family, more surprise-siblings in a sense. Surprises, changes, and unexpected life directions seemed to be the name of the game. I decided that I better get used to it, since I never knew what might be around the corner.

CHAPTER THIRTEEN

MILES AWAY

The Escovedo Brothers were gigging in Los Angeles when Coke got a call from Carlos Santana. Carlos asked him to join his band since his regular timbale player, Chepito, needed to leave for a while. Coke and I had met Carlos and most of the original Santana band a while back when we were playing in a little San Francisco club near the Broadway Tunnel. Carlos and Chepito (Jose Chepito Areas) walked in and checked out our set. "Man, you guys sound good," Carlos said. "Come on over to where we're rehearsing when you get done." Later that night, we made it over to the garage on Mission Street that they used for a rehearsal space, and a friendship was formed. We stayed there all night, just hanging and playing with the original Santana band. They were cool guys with a lot of talent. Nobody knew then that they were about to become a sensation.

By joining Santana, Coke would finally be making real money and touring the world. While Coke was off in Europe with them, I kept our band working here and there and joined others, like Bill Courtial's top forty band that mostly played in hotel lounges.

CS80

By this time, the Escovedo family had moved to 920 East 21st Street in Oakland. It was a lower flat with two bedrooms, a front room, dining room, kitchen, bath, garage, and backyard for the kids. The rent was reasonable, and the landlord, Mr. Jurkanin, seemed like a nice guy. The neighbors upstairs–Mercy Lara and her children, Carlos, Oscar, and Diana–soon became our good friends. My practicing intrigued little Carlos, and he took up the timbales as well. Soon enough, our new home on East 21st was the new party house. This was an important house for all of us. It marked a significant transition. It's where we made new friends, new beginnings, and a new future. It's also where we welcomed a new member of the family: Zina Ann Escovedo, born November 26, 1967.

I began working with Bill Courtial five nights a week in the Holiday Inn circuit in San Mateo, across the Bay from Oakland. One night, Coke stopped by since he was back in town, just off the road with Santana. It was great to see my little brother again. He'd gotten a place in San Francisco and had a new wife, a go-go dancer named Kathy, who he'd met while performing at a San Francisco club. (It was the same club where we met Bill Graham after he came into town from New York. Coke and I were playing, and we noticed this guy on the dance floor, the only one doing New York-style salsa. Between sets, we approached him at the bar. "We were watching you dance," I said. "There aren't a lot of people with that East Coast dance style here in the Bay Area." He introduced himself as Bill Graham and explained he'd recently moved from New York. "I'm planning to go to L.A. to become an actor," he told us. After he was a manager for a lot of great musicians like Eddie Money and Carlos Santana, and after he made history as an influential Bay

Area promoter, Bill did indeed do some acting. He played Charlie "Lucky" Luciano in the film *Bugsy*. You can even catch him doing that New York-style salsa dancing in one scene.)

While I played on stage that night with Bill Courtial, I saw Coke beaming in the audience. I figured he was just excited to share some tales from the road. Little did I know, he had good news for me. During the set break, he explained that there was an opening for another percussionist. "I told Carlos to hire you," he said. "And he's going to."

"Wow," I said. I couldn't believe it. "Okay! I just have to give Bill Courtial my two weeks' notice."

Coke shook his head. "You can't. We have to be in New York in two days."

Bill was kind enough to let me leave that very night. "I won't keep you from this great opportunity," he told me. I rushed home to let Juanita know I'd be leaving for New York the next day. She was stunned, but happy, and stayed up late helping me pack. Coke gave me a tape of the show that I could listen to on my Walkman on the plane. I had a lot to learn before hitting the stage the next night at Madison Square Garden, where we'd be playing four nights in a row. At sound check, I got a feel for the show, and Coke helped me along the way.

I couldn't believe I was playing with Santana. The band, full of young musicians, some of them still in their teens, had just released their third album, and they were riding high on the sales. They were mesmerizing fans with this new mixture of Rock and Latin and had become a symbol of the Latin Rock Era. The original band members were Greg Rollie on piano, organ, and lead vocals, David Brown on bass, Michael Shrieve on drums, Chepito Areas on timbales, Michael Carabello on congas, and, of course, Carlos Santana on guitar. They got their start at the Fillmore in San Francisco, where Bill Graham booked bands. It was the 1960s, the time of flower children, peace activists, free love, and psychedelics. It seemed like Latin people in the

Bay Area were looking for a new sound and a new hero. Carlos Santana was it.

The band was a co-op then. Everyone shared in the music writing and the profits. A few of their friends became managers. But too much pleasure and not enough business doesn't always work out well. And eventually the band would be impacted. Carlos was impacted the most.

The band line-up changed a little when I got there–Coke on timbales and me on congas. I'd never performed in front of so many people before. Going from little club dates to Madison Square Garden was a huge leap. To play in this kind of venue with a band I'd never been with was scary. Before we went on, I was trying to look cool backstage, wondering if anyone else could tell how nervous I was. Then the announcer gave us the standard Santana intro: "Ladies and gentleman, please welcome, from the rolling hills of San Francisco...Santana!" The applause was thunderous. When I walked out, I was stunned by the size of the crowd. The place was massive, and every seat was filled. The first song, *Batuka*, opened with a conga pattern before Carlos and the rest of the band come in. And tonight, I was the conga player. As the lights came on, and we got ready to start, the magnitude of it really hit me: *I* was the first thing the audience would hear–*my* rhythm. I looked down at my conga heads and then at my shaking hands. I felt the warmth of the spotlight, and I started. I had to do my best, impress the band, and earn my place. So I played as hard and as fast as I could. I played well. But with all my determination and passion, I cut my hand on the conga drum. They bandaged me up, but it was extremely painful to play that way. I'd never injured my hand before, and I couldn't believe I'd done it on my first night with Santana, at Madison Square Garden.

On the second night, my hand was still hurting. I couldn't hit the drum as hard as before, and I knew this wasn't sitting well with the band. I noticed a young conga player, Mingo Lewis, on the side of the stage. He hung out with the band and sometimes sat in at sound check and rehearsals. Since Carlos knew my hand was still hurting, and he liked the way Mingo played, he asked him to play the show also. Mingo came along with us to the next city as well, to help me with the congas since I was injured, and eventually he was an official addition to the band.

We went on to tour the United States, Europe, and Puerto Rico. Sometimes Chepito and Carabello joined us. I loved that we were playing for such a mixed crowd–people of color and lots of white people too. It was so cool looking out into the crowd and seeing those smiling faces. It was like they were hypnotized by the sound of Latin percussion, something many people hadn't heard before. Carlos was really able to break down that barrier.

There were some crazy, crazy times. We had a few days off in Puerto Rico before we were to play in San Juan, so the promoter wanted to give us a nice little mini-vacation. "You guys are working hard," he said. "So I want to let you rest on the island." We boarded a small plane and flew to a huge home. It was like a plantation house–with four stories and balconies all around each level. Every room was big and beautifully decorated. A soft ocean breeze drifted in through the open windows. "You guys can stay for free," he said. "There's a cook, a housekeeper, horses to ride, anything you want. And you're by the beach. Enjoy!" We were blown away. "The only thing I'd like you to do is play for the armed forces on the island."

When we showed up to play for them, it looked just like a scene from one of those old black and white movies–the army guys in uniform, holding their canteens. They were so welcoming, encouraging us to play anything we felt like, so grateful that we'd come to entertain them. They gathered around us, and we played some of our usual songs and lots of improvised tunes. It was casual and fun, like a big jam session.

Back at the house, as great as all that luxury and free time was, by the third day, everybody was bored to death.

We were all so young, and we were used to the city, with its action, lights, and noise. All this down time was getting old. So when the promoter heard how restless the guys were getting, he flew in a bunch of prostitutes. And then, everybody got happy again. But I left, eager to explore the city. I went into San Juan and walked along the cobblestone streets, exploring the casinos, the restaurants, the bars. I also bought a few outfits, since my luggage was lost, and I'd been wearing Michael Shrieve's clothes.

The gig in Puerto Rico was at night in the Roberto Clemente Stadium. They created a huge stage on the field, and they built it really high up. They also set up a fence around the stage to prevent the crowd from getting too close. "Going to be wild," one of the stage techs told me in broken English while we were sound-checking. "People excited for Santana." At first, everything started out normally. "Ladies and gentleman, please welcome, from the rolling hills of San Francisco…Santana!" I opened *Batuka* with the usual conga rhythm, but when I hit the drums, they bounced. And they kept bouncing every time I hit the skins, even when I tried not to hit that hard. The stage had been assembled too loosely, and we were so high up that it just didn't support the equipment. But the crowd wasn't picky. They didn't notice my bouncing congas since they were too busy screaming, cheering, clapping, and dancing. They were getting closer and closer to the fence, and soon they were pressing up so tightly against the fence that it began to move too. By the third song, the stage was starting to tilt. And by the fourth song, it was swaying back and forth. The crowd had knocked down the fence, and they were now charging the stage. We tried to keep playing, pretending we weren't terrified that the stage might collapse beneath our feet. I looked around at the other guys and saw they were just as freaked out as me. By now, people were all over the stage. Security was busy throwing people off stage, but they were outnumbered. The promoter cut our set short since things were getting far too out of hand, and someone was bound to get hurt. We scrambled down the stairs, hopped into the security vehicle, and took off. We could hear the crowd booing far into the distance.

CHAPTER FOURTEEN

LA PIEDRA DEL SOL

When the tour was done, my brother and I were eager to keep our momentum going. Coke made a lot of contacts with promoters and producers while he was out with Santana, so he thought it would be a good time to start up a new band with a new name and go after the big bucks. "It's time," he said. "We can call all the good musicians we know, have auditions, and just do it!"

"What would we call ourselves?" I asked him.

"I don't know. Something cool."

"Yeah, we need a name that nobody else has. Something really different."

And then, inspired by a book about Aztecs and Mayan artwork, a name popped into my head. "Let's call ourselves 'Azteca'."

Coke gave me a wide grin. "I like it."

In that moment, the new band was created. At least in theory. Naming the band was the easy part. Now we had to begin the process of finding musicians, writing songs, rehearsing, and preparing a showcase for record companies. Coke secured a rehearsal space at San Francisco's Kabuki Hotel and Convention Center. His wife introduced him to the facility's manager, Archie Hiroto, who generously agreed to let us have our showcase in the theatre. Word got around about our big audition, and tons of folks showed up. Coke was especially thrilled by the turnout. Sometimes I wonder if Coke was intent on creating an extraordinary band because his ego was a little bruised after Santana let him go once Chepito had returned.

Our next step was to feature our music at a showcase. We set out to combine different musical elements–Latin, jazz, rock–within a large orchestra. We wanted to expand Latin rock, take it beyond the blues and Afro-Cuban base. We wanted the blues and the Afro-Cuban sound, of course, but we wanted to integrate some soul, some funk, and some jazz. Coke wanted Michael Shrieve on drums for the showcase, and even Carlos came by for a few rehearsals to support. We had George Maribus on electric piano, Flip Nunez on organ, and George DiQuattro on acoustic piano. The horn section was Tom Harrell on trumpet, Mel Martin and Bob Ferriera on saxophone, Jules Rowell and Pat O'Hara on trombone, Paul Jackson on bass, Lenny White on drums after Shrieve was back on the road with Carlos, Neal Schon and Jim Vincent on guitar, Victor Pantoja on congas, Errol Knowles, Rico Reyes, Wendy Hass, and myself on vocals. They were all great musicians who Coke and I had played with through the years. And more than that, they were great friends.

The band's musical style came from the combination of phenomenal players with diverse musical backgrounds. The Latin rhythms were prominent. At the same time, a lot of the guys came from a jazz background, so we integrated lots of jazz harmonies and melodies. But we wanted to keep the Latin rock going as well as R&B. Since all of us, as a co-op, were bringing in our own music and our own ideas, each song was a true collaboration, and each had its own unique layers of contribution from each of us.

After a few weeks of intensive rehearsals, we were ready to showcase our band. We contacted all the record labels, promoters, talent agents, and producers we knew. We ran ads in papers, put up posters, and made phone calls. We hustled. On the night of the showcase, there was a big crowd. As Coke and I looked out into the audience, we recognized a few industry folks, but for the most part, we didn't know who was who. We just hoped there were enough record people there, not just fans and fellow musicians. The band was well rehearsed, amped up, confident, and ready to impress. The show was fantastic. Everything went as planned. Better than planned, really. We got loud applause and lots of visitors backstage offering praise and congratulations. Many record executives were backstage too, slipping us their cards and asking us to give them a call. Coke and I were beaming. Folks were enthusiastic about our sound and the socio-political message of our lyrics.

"We did it," I told him.

"Azteca is born," he said, flashing a big smile and giving me a hug. His vision was coming to life.

CHAPTER FIFTEEN

NEW DAY IS ON THE RISE

It was time to discuss our next move. Coke thought we should make the band a co-op band, like Santana, so that we all shared in the losses and the profits. We called a meeting a few days later and decided we should form a committee within the band–a smaller group elected to conduct the future meetings and vote on important decisions. I was to be treasurer, Coke was our president and producer, and George Maribus, Lenny White, and Mel Martin were the other committee members. Our first meeting was with Electra Records in Los Angeles. "Play it cool, Peter," Coke told me during our flight down to L.A. "We don't want to jump at the first offer." Electra proposed a good offer which we took back to the band. Clive Davis from Columbia Records also expressed interest. We took that back to the band too. We were getting inundated with offers. We had lots of committee meetings–in Oakland, in San Francisco, and sometimes at Neil's house, across the bay in Sausalito. It was time for some legal advice. An entertainment lawyer advised us to take the Columbia offer. Clive Davis met us at Neil's house to seal the deal. Clive was the big-wig within the company. He had a great track record, having discovered and promoted bands like The Pointer Sisters and Earth, Wind, & Fire, so we were excited to work with him.

Clive flew us out to London where he would present us as part of a Columbia Records new act preview. He was making a splash, showing the world CBS' new direction by featuring us with the Pointer Sisters, Earth, Wind, & Fire, and Weather Report. Clive told us we could order anything we wanted from the hotel since Columbia was picking up the tab. Coke came to my room, and we ordered filet mignon, champagne, and sundaes. We were giggling like little kids. We'd come a long way from sharing a tiny cot in that little Oakland apartment and enduring all those lonely nights at Saint Vincent's Home for Boys.

In the hotel conference room, I was given $50,000 in cash as an advance payment. I was so nervous carrying all that money with me. When I got home, I dropped my luggage, quickly gave my wife and kids hugs and gifts, and then immediately raced over to the bank to deposit all that money. During the next week, we opened a small business office, hired a secretary, and began the business of Azteca. Next, we signed a booking deal with the William Morris Agency, where Peter Shields was our agent. As soon as the new Azteca record was released, he booked a lot of shows for us. Peter took good care of us and became a good friend.

In September of 1972, we recorded our first album at Columbia Records in San Francisco. Every song was an original composition written by the band members. The energy in the studio felt electric. We all knew we had something special. Our music and lyrics were a reflection of the culture and the times–politically and socially. But the songs still seem to hold up today. Our intentions were pure, and I think that made the music timeless.

We hired Bruce Steinberg to design our record cover, asking for a design based on the Aztec calendar. Bruce came up with the idea of using the calendar as a band logo, placing instruments in and around it. We loved the final design. It represented us perfectly. These were Coke's words on the back of the album:

Azteca is all our hopes, ambitions, aspirations. However, above all, it is our music and our lives. When I first thought of forming Azteca, I had a dream of playing with musicians who were serious and who would put music above all else. No egos, no superstars, no plastic personalities. Our motive is not financial gain, for we are grateful for our gift. We feel our music is an art and not a product. Just good music from good musicians. I believe my dream has come true, and I hope you will agree after you have listened to Azteca.

Everything Coke wrote was accurate. We all collaborated and stayed true to our collective gift. We put the art before the business.

Columbia records started advance promotion with ads in all the music trades, and as soon as the record was released, things started to happen. Our agent got the ball rolling by booking a few tours. We opened for Stevie Wonder on a college tour and later opened for The Temptations. We studied their stage presence, their musicianship, and their professionalism. It was great to perform in large venues, and we started to develop a following. The Latin rock music scene was getting bigger, and we had a lot of Latin fans. Since our William Morris contract stipulated a certain number of performances per year, we started working in some strange places–small towns and small clubs. We weren't yet big enough to headline, but we were happy to take whatever the agency gave us.

Our first big venue was the San Diego Padres baseball stadium. As we drove down, we couldn't stop talking about what it might be like, only stopping our chatter to sing along to Stevie Wonder, whose music we blasted the whole way there. He was one of many artists we used to listen to for writing inspiration. I stared out the window onto the long highway, Stevie's soothing voice in the background. It felt like something really special was about to happen–headlining at such a big concert, in a huge baseball stadium, and in San Diego with so many Latins in the crowd. And sure enough, the show went off without a hitch. We were a hit.

Despite all our hard work and all the great feedback, we kept coming back from the road owing more than we made. Bills were coming in from all over the place–flights, rental cars, truck rentals, hotel bills, office rent, and payroll for road crew and our secretary. We never seemed to have enough to pay the band. We were willing to sacrifice in the beginning because we were looking ahead, committed to doing whatever we could to make this collective project work and hoping things would get better. But the band kept growing, whether we intended for it to grow or not. There were so many musicians hanging out backstage and at rehearsals. "We want to join," they'd say. "Okay, come on in," one of us would say. Eventually we had multiple roadies and many managers and countless hangers-on. It was a come-one-come-all vibe.

Soon enough, it was time to start getting our music together to record our second album, *Pyramid of the Moon*. The vibe wasn't the same as it was when we recorded the first time. Things were changing within the band. Some band members were becoming concerned about the way business was run. There were some shady characters hanging around, and money wasn't always accounted for. Eventually, Lenny quit the band and went back to New York. Before he left, he was able to play on a few of the new record's songs. John Brink and Paul Jackson performed on several songs as well. The other bass players were Tom Rutley and Tony Juncale. Paul later moved to Japan, where he still lives. Neal Schon played on one song, but he didn't stay with Azteca as he rejoined the Santana band. Then we hired Bill Courtial.

Despite the internal shifts, we managed to finish the second album. I think it was another great one, another one that's endured the test of time.

ᏮᏋᎧ

Other changes are difficult to explain and painful to revisit. They're what led to our ultimate downfall. Drugs were a norm in the music industry. Our band was no exception. Not every band member was using drugs, but there was enough drug use going on to negatively impact everyone. Money was going to drug suppliers, and it seemed like these shady guys were around us all the time. It affected our relationships, our business, and our music. Our debt was growing, and things were really falling apart.

As a co-op, we all had a voice, a vote, an opinion that mattered. But Coke was the president, the leader, the producer, and, I'm sorry to say, the main cause of the band's eventual destruction. A meeting was called to discuss what we could do to save the future of Azteca. Everyone voted on whether or not Coke would have to leave the band and surrender his leadership, let go of his questionable business ties, and stop his negative "friends" from bringing in the drugs. Only one person voted to keep him: me. This band was his dream, and he'd created this project from nothing. And he was my brother.

I pleaded with them. "He'll change, you guys. We can't go on without him. It's not right."

They shook their heads. Nobody believed me. To be very honest, deep down I didn't believe me either. Coke had crossed a line of no return.

The band tried to move on without Coke. But without him—his charisma, his talent, his unique energy—the record company lost interest. We lost our booking agent and our contract with Columbia Records. Meanwhile, Coke signed a record deal with Mercury Records and recorded a few solo albums. I'd mostly been singing and playing some hand percussion in Azteca, but once Coke left, I moved over to timbales. I knew I couldn't do the job that Coke was doing– he was a much better player. I tried to keep it together and find other musicians to join the band, but we'd lost our foundation. The spirit of the band was fundamentally deflated.

I kept trying to keep us going, nonetheless. We hired a new manager, Barry Hamilton, son of the great jazz drummer Chico Hamilton. We weren't getting a lot of work, and soon the original members were jumping ship. Tom Harrell moved to New York and later became a famous jazz trumpet player. We couldn't afford three keyboard players, so Flip Nunez moved to Hawaii and began working in the hotel lounges as a solo piano player. George Di Quattro formed a small band in San Francisco. Several members passed away: George Maribus, Rico Reyes, and Pat O'Hara. The remaining members were Don Grusin on piano, Tom Rutley on bass, Bill Courtial on guitar, Mel Martin and Bob Ferreira on saxophone, Eddie Henderson on trumpet, Victor Pantoja on congas, Terry Bozio on drums, Jules Rowell on trombone, and Wendy Hass and Errol Knowles on vocals. We started working on a third album with hopes that our new manager would get us a new record deal with Atlantic Records. We recorded a few songs in Los Angeles and gave the tapes to Barry to shop for a new deal. But nothing came of our efforts. Without a record deal and with so few gigs, more members gave up on the dream. I eventually scraped up enough money to buy the tapes back from the recording studios since they hadn't yet been paid.

◌୪༽◌

Azteca was losing steam, and our gigs were few and far between, but there was one very special one. Sheila made her Azteca debut in San Francisco at a big event for Mayor George Moscone. She had begged me to let her play that day since our percussionist, Victor, was sick. I initially said no, worried that while she surely had some chops, she was too young and just not experienced enough with our music. But Juanita saw the excitement in Sheila's eyes, and she insisted I give our daughter a shot. Sheila blew me and the crowd away that day. She seemed to blow herself away too. Her solo brought us both to tears. I had no idea what an amazing player she'd become. Backstage after the show, I knew what she was about to tell me. "Pops, I want to go on the road with you." I didn't want to say yes, but I couldn't deny what she already knew.

After that fateful performance, her life direction changed. She went from being a girl who played music to a musician with a clear career focus. I agreed to have her join me on tour in Columbia. It was a big decision, taking my 15-year-old on the road to another country and surrounding her with the craziness of the music scene. Juanita, once again, encouraged me. "It's a once in a lifetime experience," she said. "Look how happy she is playing with you." And so we bought our daughter her first plane ticket. My little girl was suddenly my bandmate and touring buddy. She was officially a professional musician, and I couldn't believe I was giving my blessing. When we played our first show in Bogotá, Columbia, in the middle of a bullring, the crowd went crazy. They were in awe watching this teenage girl throw down. That bullring will never be the same. Even those bulls had to sit back.

When we got back home, I realized there'd been a buzz developing around town. "Who's this young girl on the congas? Pete's daughter…Coke's niece…." Before they saw Sheila play, she was like some kind of urban legend. I decided it was time to sit her down and give her a serious talk about the importance of staying strong in the music business. I reminded her that a lot of guys weren't going to welcome a female drummer/percussionist. She did indeed have to deal with a lot of men who resented her. But most of them got humbled pretty quickly once they saw her professionalism and talent, once they realized she wasn't just a pretty face trying to play a man's instrument. It was *her* instrument. She schooled all the doubters.

Sheila kept playing with Azteca and with me in whatever little gigs I could find. We hustled. Sometimes we didn't make any money once we'd paid the band. Or we'd make just enough for a burger and milk shake after the gig.

Meanwhile, my boys were getting to be good players too. The truth is, despite my attempts at steering them toward a steadier profession, Sheila, Juan, and Peter Michael, ever since they were little, had never been able to stay off my instruments, whether at home or at a venue. I'd walk away for one minute and come back to find them in their own little jam session. While they were into all the normal things their peers were doing, like hanging with friends and playing sports, their favorite thing to do was to absorb the sounds of all the musicians in the front room. They especially loved coming with me to group homes where we played for and with the children. It was my favorite way of giving back, knowing that if musicians had come to Saint Vincent's Home for Boys way back when, it would've given Coke and me a lot of inspiration. My kids had joined bands and formed their own. Their first paid gig was a *quinceañera*. They were over the moon because they were getting paid, $5 each.

Juan and Peter Michael became Azteca's roadies, jumping on the instruments before and after sound check. They let me tell them what to do, but they weren't so happy with their big sister bossing them around. They never asked to join the band, but once I noticed how good they'd gotten, I invited them to play. First I had them keep time for us on the cow bell—one of the best ways to learn timing. Eventually they were on percussion, right next to me and Sheila. Their talent snuck up on me. They went from being those little wide-eyed toddlers, refusing to go to bed because the music in the front room was too exciting, to my musical equals.

Since their hobby was becoming their passion, and since they were working with me more and more, I thought it was important to give all three of them some rules and some advice. I sat them all down one day. "Be respectful. That's number one." They nodded. "Always show up early," I told them. "Whether it's rehearsal, sound check, or show time. Be there early. On time is already late."

"Got it, Pops," said Sheila.

"And dress to impress," I said.

"That one we already know," Juan said.

Sheila nodded. "Yeah, we got that one down."

"Pops, we *are* your kids," said Peter Michael.

And thus we had the beginnings of what years later would be the E. Family band.

INTERLUDE

COUNTING DAYS: STAGES AND PAGES FROM THE ROAD

Being on tour with the Santana band was always a blur of planes and buses, hotel lobbies and hotel rooms, sound checks and jams, applause and celebration. I started journaling in the summer of 1978, and here I'll share some journal entries from those days of travel, little snippets from the road. As I read them now, with years of hindsight of course, it's clear that while I was living my dream—as a professional musician in a great band—I had trouble fully appreciating it. These journal pages are colored with a sadness and a longing. I was playing with extraordinary musicians, experiencing new cultures, making great music and great friends, all while getting paid to express myself creatively. I hadn't anticipated the great cost that came along with the increased pay. I was missing the one thing that mattered most, the one dream I had already accomplished without really knowing it: my home and my family. I had chosen Juanita, surely because I knew she could help me create the kind of family cohesion I'd longed for my whole life. While on the road, I was missing out on the family life I'd always dreamed of. I was missing out on my kids' milestones. They weren't there with me to share in these new experiences, and so it all felt incomplete. Yes, music is my passion, and I still get to live out my professional and creative dreams on the stage. But as for my heart, that's at home with my family.

June 27, 1978

Why journal now? Maybe it's because so many good things happened to me the past few years. It's about time I start keeping some kind of record of my life. For posterity. To remember all the blessings.

I'm making an attempt to get myself up and going. Sheila is still on the road with George Duke. I spoke with her yesterday, and she sounds very homesick. She's been away a long time and hasn't seen the new house that we just moved into.

We're all busy trying to get the place in shape. It's a great house, and I'm enjoying this new home. We moved here June 15, 1978, and after being at 920 E. 21st for over 12 years, this was a big move. But we were due for a change, and I'm very happy with the way things turned out. Everything is going smooth except for making a living on our own, even though Sheila and I have two albums out. We still can't get to that next level.

That's mainly why she's been working with George, and me with Carlos. Maybe by July we can all be together for my birthday and Peter Michael and Patrice's housewarming as well.

July 8, 1978

Well, here I am in Hollywood. We got here around 11:30 this morning. Had something to eat after checking into the Sunset Marquis Hotel. Got Sheila's favorite room: 111.

Went to the studio to record with Carlos, which is why we're here. Left around 7 p.m. for dinner and then back to the studio. Back to the hotel around 12:20 a.m. Pretty tired. Sleepy. Been up all day. The first night away from home is always the worst. It was great being home for a while. I miss it already.

July 11, 1978

I'm on my way back to Los Angeles. I was home for two days to see the family. Coke and his friend Dennis hung out with me in L.A. Had a great time. Went to see Johnny Nelson at Candela's Club. The next day had lunch at Rudy's Pasta House in East L.A. and later hung out at the club Virginia's.

The best part was seeing my dad. My brother Javier brought him over to the hotel. We didn't have a chance to talk much because they got there pretty late and had to get back to Huntington Beach. It was great to see Pops again. Looking at him now is like seeing myself when I reach his age. God willing. As far as the recording session goes, we've just been putting down basic tracks. Graham Lear on drums, David Margen on bass, Chris Rhyne on piano, Greg Walker on vocals, Raul Rekow, Armando Perraza, and myself on percussion.

July 12, 1978

Soon it will be my birthday, and it seems like time is going by so fast. Just when I'm getting used to being 42, suddenly I'm 43.

Well, that's something you can't stop: Father Time.

Sheila will be home in a few days, and it will be so nice to see her again.

Fantasy finally sent us our release, which I figured was coming sooner or later as the two albums didn't sell as much as they wanted. So they let us go. I really can't complain because our names are getting out there, and people know who we are. We have been fortunate. We have a nice place to live, and the family is well and happy.

We just want to make it on our own instead of working for other people. I haven't given up hope, and I still believe in what we do. I just wish it would happen soon. It will. It has to.

July 16, 1978

Back to L.A. to finish up the recording and take photos for the cover. I think Inner Secrets will do well. This means we'll be headed back out on the road to promote the new album.

July 25, 1978

Well, we are all at home for a little while, just enjoying the new house and being together while we can because it won't be for long. Sheila bought her first car. A 1974 Volvo. She was so happy to have her own car. She had to leave for L.A. to play at the Roxie and then at the Oakland Coliseum. In the meantime, I was doing Day on the Green at the Oakland Stadium with Carlos and the Rolling Stones.

August 2, 1978

Went to L.A. again to play for the CBS Convention at the Century Plaza Hotel. Went to see Sheila at the Roxie. Took the whole Santana band with me.

Went to the Hong Kong Bar to see Willie Bobo and Victor Pantoja. We went to a party with Joe Cocker and friends and partied until 6 a.m.

Had to leave the next day, but I ended up staying a few more days just to hang out with Pantoja.

Finally got home Sunday.

August 11, 1978

I've been rehearsing with Coke and his new band for a gig at The Pasta House in L.A. Sheila is also in the band. The gig is later on this month for three nights.

The gig with Coke at the Pasta House was so much fun. The night we opened there wasn't much of a crowd, but it was still fun. Louis Miranda came by and sat in. The last set was just about over when Tito Puente came to see us straight from the airport. After the gig, we all went to his hotel and hung out for a while. The next night, the club was packed, even though Tito, Eddie Palmieri, and Fajardo were playing at the Palladium in Hollywood.

Got home the next night around 11:30 p.m. Juanita picked me up at the Oakland Airport. We went straight to the gig where Tito was playing. Sheila and Gibby Ross sat in. They all sounded great.

Tried to rest on Sunday, but we had a lot of company at the house, as always. So it wasn't until late at night that I started packing for my flight to Detroit.

September 3, 1978

It's about 10:30 a.m., and I'm in Chicago about to leave for Atlanta. Our first four days in Detroit were spent rehearsing the new songs from the new album. The first gig was okay, but we sounded better the next time at a club called The Beginning, which is owned by drummer Bobby Colomby from the band Chicago.

After Atlanta, it's back home for a few days. It's getting harder and harder to be away from the family. I miss all of them, and it's always hard for me to sleep when I'm away from home. I won't be home until Friday. Then we leave for Santa Barbara for one gig and then come back home to play the Greek Theatre on Sunday. This traveling is starting to get me down. But it comes with the job. And it's a job I always wanted. Music…it's my life.

September 9, 1978

Just got back from Santa Barbara where we played outdoors. It was a smaller venue, and the weather was nice and warm. We left on Friday, which was Juanita's birthday, so we didn't get a chance to celebrate.

Sheila leaves tomorrow for Brazil with George. She gets back on Friday. There will be a family reunion, but I'll have to miss that because I leave again on Friday for New Mexico.

Coke is in the studio working on some new music. I wish I could start on my stuff soon.

I had to be at Winterland for the taping of Midnight Special. Arrived there at 3 p.m. and left around 12:30 a.m. We had to play the same three songs over and over again. Now that was a job.

September 26, 1978

It's Tuesday night, and I'm trying to get my stuff together because I'm leaving again on another

Santana road trip. A three-week run. And I just got back from the road Sunday night. We played Monterey on the 22nd–two shows with Eddie Money. We flew there from San Francisco then back to San Francisco and then caught a flight to Eureka.

Got on a bus for a six-hour drive to Chico. Played a show there and then rode the bus back home. Man, was I ever tired.

I keep asking Santana management for a raise because I'm working my butt off. I told them if I don't get a raise then I'll have to give my notice. We'll see what happens.

October 5, 1978

We're on the East Coast doing college shows. A place called Champagne, wherever that is.

Left Champagne on Wednesday 11:30 a.m., changed planes in Chicago, and arrived in Columbus, Ohio, around 3:30 p.m. Got settled, had some dinner, and then went back to my room to try to catch up on some sleep. As usual, I haven't been sleeping well. So I try to take a nap for a few hours in the daytime. Took my clothes to the laundry and went down to the bar for a drink. So much for my day off.
It's been about a week since we left home. Two more weeks to go. Sound check at 5:30 p.m. and show time at 8 p.m.

After the show, Raul had a party in his room. There was also a good band at the hotel lounge, so I hung out there until 3 a.m.

October 6, 1978

Left Columbus and drove to Toledo. Got a letter from Juanita and the kids that warmed my heart. Checked into hotel. Sound check and gig. Same ol' same...

October 7, 1978

Left Toledo at 11 a.m. and drove to Kent, Ohio. It was our worst gig yet. Seemed like we were all tired. So much for Kent, Ohio.

October 8, 1978

Left Kent and drove to Dayton, Ohio. It was a long trip. Five hours. Sound check and then gig The band sounded much better.

October 9, 1978

Left Dayton, Ohio at 11 a.m. and caught a flight to New York. Arrived around 1:30 p.m. The weather in New York was nice. A little cool but the sun was out. Drove about an hour to Passaic, New Jersey. Sound check, gig, hotel, and bed. Really missing Juanita and the kids.

October 10, 1978

Left New Jersey at 12:30 p.m. and drove to Albany. Same routine.

October 11, 1978

Left Albany and drove to Providence, Rhode Island. Another five-hour drive. It was our day off. Not much to do. Just clean clothes, hang out at the bar, drink too much. Went to bed. Slept late today and had a chance to rest. But for once I slept really well, maybe because I drank so much. I have to cool it with that. Enough is enough.

Went to have breakfast and then went for a walk with Armando. Time for sound check and the gig.

Had to pack after the show because our luggage was going on the small truck, and we were flying on a small chartered plane. So, early to bed for the 8:30 a.m. call.

October 13, 1978

Left Providence at 9:30 a.m. The flight wasn't that bad considering that I don't like flying in small planes. We arrived in Endicott, New York. Just an hour flight. Tonight, another gig. I just realized it's Friday the 13th. What a day to fly in a small plane.

October 14, 1978

Today was the craziest day so far. It had to be the longest and most miserable day of all. To start, it was raining cats and dogs when we left Endicott this morning on our way to Dartmouth. This time, the flight in that little plane was terrible. I was really scared and started to get sick. We couldn't land in Dartmouth because of the heavy rain and fog. So we had to land at another airport in Concord. I thought for sure we were going to crash, and I imagined Juanita and the kids hearing about it on TV. But thanks to God, we landed safe but not so sound. We had to take cabs to Dartmouth, an hour and a half away. We had no hotel because of the football game between Dartmouth and Yale. Every hotel was booked. We had to stay at the gig the entire time. Had to play in our traveling clothes.

After the gig, we boarded a plane again to fly to Portland, Maine. Most of the band refused to get back on the plane, including Carlos and the road manager. I was so tired and worn out that I decided to take the plane. It was the shortest route, and I just couldn't wait to get there, take a shower, and go to bed. I chose the flight and got to bed at 2 a.m. Man, what a day. Only two more days to go.

October 16, 1978

Arrived in New York at 10:30 a.m. Sound Check at 5:30 p.m. First show at 8:30 p.m. The Bottom

Line Club is a small spot, and the band was very loud. We're used to playing in larger venues, so we have to adjust. Second show was much better. Al Jarreau, Ruben Blades, and a lot of other musicians came by to check us out. Glad it was our last gig. Going home tomorrow. Can't wait to see the family.

October 23, 1978

The days at home went by too quick. I did nothing but rest and enjoy my time with family. Saturday the 21st was our 22nd wedding anniversary. We weren't sure how to celebrate. We thought about going to Reno or Tahoe but decided just to stay in town, have dinner, and hit the night clubs in San Francisco. We ate at Sinbad's restaurant and then went to see Joe Williams at the Mocambo. Then went to see Cal Tjader at Cristo's. After that, we went to the Reunion to see John Santos and Tipica Cienfuegos. We ended up at Juanita's brother Nick's house for his birthday party. The whole family was there. I got completely drunk. They said I had a great time. The next day I cooled out, and later we took Zina to the movies.

So it was almost time to get back out on the road again. They made our departure date earlier than scheduled. I wasn't too happy about leaving home again so soon. This trip would be a long one. I won't be back until December, so I'll be missing Thanksgiving and Zina's birthday. I might miss Sheila's birthday as well. I guess this is the price you pay for being a traveling musician.

The boys are doing well. Juan bought Johnny Ray's '66 Riviera. Peto is still Mr. G.Q. And Sheila is in and out of town with George. I just worry about Juanita and Zina, always hoping they'll be okay while I'm gone.

We left San Francisco Airport at 7:30 p.m. Juanita drove David Margen and me to the airport. I said goodbye to all the kids at home. Zina didn't want to go to the airport. I think she was feeling bad because I was leaving again.

The trip to London was long and uncomfortable. Ten hours. Tomorrow we have another day off, so I'll probably go shopping at Kingston Market and King's Road. We'll be here rehearsing, and then our first show is Monday. I hope the days go by fast. I miss home already.

November 2, 1978

We arrived in Stafford, England, about an hour ago. We left London this afternoon at 12:30 p.m. The bus ride was about four hours long. We have the night off, so I'm just hanging in my room.

The first week in London wasn't so bad. The first couple of days I went shopping and sightseeing in between rehearsals. I went to see Elvin Jones at Ronnie Scott's. I went to see Star Wars at the movie theatre. And I called home a lot.

Our first show was at Wembley Empire Pool. We got better as we went along. We hadn't performed *in a while, so it took us some time to warm up. After the show, CBS and the promoters took us to a Greek restaurant where you can break dishes. It was great fun. CBS presented Carlos with a platinum album. Wednesday night was our last show and our best in London. Herbie Hancock sat in with us.*

Next stop, Manchester, England. Only 39 more days to go. Missing home.

November 5, 1978

Got up at 11 a.m. and decided to stay in my room until show time. We play two shows tonight then leave tomorrow by plane to Brussels, Belgium. Today is Sunday, so I'll call home and talk to the family. I'm starting to get really homesick. 36 more days to go.

November 6, 1978

Left Manchester at 8:30 a.m. and arrived in Brussels at 11 a.m. Nothing to do but stay in my room again and rest.

November 7, 1978

Got up early this morning and went jogging with Carlos. Later walked around with Armando. Went to dinner after the show with the band. CBS gave Carlos a double gold album for Moonflower. Leave in the morning for Berlin.

November 8, 1978

Wake-up call was 8:30 a.m. Didn't get much sleep. Changed planes in Frankfurt and arrived in Berlin at 3 p.m. Went to the gig at 6:30 p.m. Catching a cold. Feel terrible. We leave again in the morning for Hamburg, Germany. 33 more days to go.

November 9, 1978

Spent most of the day traveling. Weather is foggy. Flight was delayed. Played two shows in Hamburg.

November 10, 1978

Day off. But had to catch two planes. Arrived in Goteborg, Sweden, at 4:30 p.m. Got mail from Juanita and the kids. Their words always cheer me up. Zina sent me the sweetest note about how much she missed me. She drew a picture of herself crying into a bucket of tears. That was hard to take. Time for bed.

November 11, 1978

Had breakfast in my room. Went for a walk. Had rehearsal today at 4:30 p.m. One show tonight. Still have a cold but feeling better.

November 12, 1978

Left Gothenburg this morning at 11 a.m. Traveled by bus to Lund, Sweden. Took about four hours. Had to be at sound check at 4:30 p.m. Gig tonight.

Didn't play well. Feeling tired. Called home and talked to Juanita and Zina. The other kids were out and about. Sometimes I wonder just how hard it is for them having me gone. They have no idea what it's like to be so far away from home. I miss them terribly.

November 13, 1978

Today was one of those long and tiring days. We left Lund at 11:30 a.m. and drove by bus to Malmo where we boarded a hydrofoil boat to Copenhagen. Then caught a flight to Oslo, Norway. We'll be at the gig at 6:30 p.m. Wow, what a day.

November 14, 1978

Flew from Oslo, Norway, to Copenhagen. Had a press conference at the hotel. Two shows tonight. 27 more days to go.

November 15, 1978

Slept late. Day off. Went to dinner. Saw Liza Minnelli. Talked with Victor Paz, who's in her band. Going to bed. Leave again in the morning. Cold is getting better. Just tired from travelling. Hope to get my second wind for the next half of the tour.

November 16, 1978

Left Copenhagen at 9 a.m. Took the bus to Bremen. The hotel is one of those old buildings surrounded by a large park and lake. Very beautiful. Picturesque.

Sound check at 5 p.m. Stayed at the gig and played one show. After show, went to bed. Leaving in the morning for Holland. 25 days to go.

November 17, 1978

Couldn't get to sleep last night and don't know why. Maybe just tired of being on the road. Got up at 7 a.m. and drove to Hamburg by bus. Caught a plane to Holland. Two more shows tonight. Tired. Going to bed. Leave for Frankfurt tomorrow morning.

November 19, 1978

Arrived in Frankfurt at 2 p.m. Show time at 7:30 p.m. After the show, I didn't go to dinner with CBS and the band. Too tired. Got another gold album for Moonflower. 23 more days to go.

Today is Sunday, and I'm excited to hear from home. Arrived here in Zurich, Switzerland, at 2:30 p.m. Have an early show so just grabbed a bite to eat and went to the gig. I'm feeling better, so I played a lot better. Had a chance to talk to Bill Graham about him helping Sheila and me out with a record deal. So I have my hopes up again. Time will tell.

November 20, 1978

We arrived in Stuttgart, Germany. Took a short nap as soon as I got to the hotel. Had to be ready at 5:30 p.m. The gig was an hour and a half away by bus. Another show down. 21 more days to go.

November 21, 1978

Today was a traveling day, and we have a day off. We are here in Dortmund, Germany. Sent a card to Zina for her birthday.

November 22, 1978

Slept really late. Got up around 1 in the afternoon. Had to leave at 3 p.m. for the 6 p.m. gig. After the show, Raul, Armando, and I hung out until 1 a.m. at a disco club around the corner from the hotel. Leaving in the morning for Passau, Germany. 19 more days to go.

November 23, 1978

Today is Thanksgiving, but it means nothing when you're on the road. Spent most of the day traveling even though it's our day off. We arrived in Passau around 5 p.m. Passau is by far the most beautiful place in Germany. It has three rivers that all meet together. There are boats and shops along the river bank. I wish Juanita and the kids could see all of this and be here with me.

The band had Thanksgiving dinner together, but you could tell that we were all wishing we were home with our families. Anyway, back to the disco, back to the hotel, back to bed.

November 24, 1978

Got up, had breakfast, went shopping, took some photos. Played another show. We leave for Nuremburg in the morning. 17 days to go. Can't wait to give big hugs to Juanita and the kids. I'm going to need to buy an extra suitcase just for all the presents I've bought for them.

November 25, 1978

We left Passau at 11:30 a.m. The bus ride was over three hours long. We arrived just outside of Nuremburg at 3 p.m. There was a track across from the hotel, so I went for a nice run.

The gig was one of the worst on this trip. Lousy hall, lousy sound. And we played pretty lousy too. Oh well. The crowd loved it. Rock and roll.

Tomorrow is Sunday. I'll be getting a call from home since it'll be Zina's birthday.

November 26, 1978

Another bus ride. Almost five hours. Checked into hotel. Went to gig. Sunday shows are early. Got back to hotel and waited for Juanita's call from home. The family was there to celebrate Zina's birthday. Sad to be missing it. Another milestone missed. Talked to my mom and Papa Jim.

Tomorrow we play in Stuttgart, Germany.

November 27, 1978

Another day on the bus. When we arrived in Heidelberg, it started to snow. From my hotel window, I got a great view of snow falling on the city. Looked like a movie. The gig was in Stuttgart, so we had to drive about an hour there and back. We play here on Wednesday and then go to Hannover on Thursday. We have a day off tomorrow.

November 28, 1978

Stayed in my room most of the day. Went down to eat. Got a call from Juanita. She sounds lonely. Another day gone by. 13 more to go.

November 29, 1978

Slept in as late as possible. I figured I might as well rest while I can. Played another show and then back to the hotel and back to bed.

November 30, 1978

Left Heidelberg at 11:30 a.m. Arrived in Hannover at 3 p.m. Lobby call at 6:30 p.m. Packed house. 10,000 people. Everybody played great. Leaving at 9:30 a.m. for Cologne, Germany. 11 more days to go.

December 1, 1978

After two plane rides, we arrived in Cologne at 3:30 p.m. I didn't play well on this gig. I just couldn't get into it. Maybe I'm just tired of the same old thing. Feels like it's getting worse instead of better. 10 more days to go.

December 2, 1978

Well, same old schedule. Catch a plane. Check into hotel. Play two shows here in Munich, Germany. First show was a mess. Second show a lot better. The promoter had a party for us after the show because it was our last gig in Germany. Leaving tomorrow for Paris, France.

December 3, 1978

Well, here I am in Paris. Got here at 2:30 p.m. From my room, I have a great view of the city. Went out to look for something to buy, but everything is so expensive. We will be here four or five days, so I'll get to do a lot of sightseeing.

December 8, 1978

We've been here for five days, and I tried to see as much of Paris as I could. We've been playing every night, and all the shows have been sold out. I got a chance to go to the Louvre museum. It took a whole day as there is so much to see—the Mona Lisa, Venus De Milo…so many great works of art. I'll never forget it. Went to Notre-Dame Church. It was beautiful but sort of spooky. I felt a sense of death there. I spent a lot of time shopping. I bought some stuff for the kids. Went to see the show at the Lido de Paris. Man, it was incredible. So I'm really enjoying my time here in Paris. We're playing another show for the President. It's benefitting kids in need. Then one last show before we head home.

December 9, 1978

Our last show is in Nice tomorrow night. We stay there overnight and then catch a plane back to Paris. Then a plane back home.

December 10, 1978

We arrived in Nice around 12:30 p.m. It's a little warmer here, and it sort of reminds me of Miami.

The last show was great fun. The crew threw confetti all over us on the last song. We had dinner together after the show, and I think we all drank a little too much. We said our goodbyes and got to bed around 3 a.m.

This tour is finally over.

December 11, 1978

It was a long trip from Paris to New York. Through customs. And onto our flight to San Francisco. Juanita, Sheila, Juan, Zina, and Corn were there to greet me at the airport.

Juanita had the Christmas tree up, and the house looked great for the holidays. I'm so happy to be home again. I plan on just resting.

Sheila's birthday party is coming up, so I want to be ready for that.

So what's next for the Escovedo family? I have no clue. I just thank God for getting me back home safe again.

CHAPTER SIXTEEN

SOLO TWO

During my endless hustle to keep working, getting together any combination of band members I could, I landed a weekly gig at the Reunion Club in San Francisco. Friends and fans would gather, and we slowly built a steady fan base. But, as always, the money was funny. I tried to keep my head up, telling myself and reassuring Sheila that at least we had a place to try out new songs and have some fun. I was still calling the band Azteca, but without all the original band members, none of the songs sounded the same. So we started trying out new material. One night at the Reunion, our flute player, Roger Glenn, told us that the great drummer Billy Cobham was stopping by to check us out.

After the first set, I sat down at his table to chat. He told me he was in town doing some recording, and he needed some Latin percussion on some of his songs. He wanted me and Sheila to play on the session. I told Sheila not to get too excited. "Lots of people in the industry make big promises," I warned her. "Don't get your hopes up, honey. We'll see if he actually calls."

She looked a little deflated. "Okay, Pops."

But Billy wasn't just one of those all-talk guys in the music biz. He was the real deal, a man of his word. Just a few days later, he called the house to schedule a recording session. I was really happy—not just about working with him and sharing the project with my daughter, but because she wouldn't be let down after all.

When we arrived at CBS Studios in San Francisco, we were excited to meet the other musicians. George Duke was on piano, John Scofield on guitar, and Alphonso Johnson on bass. Sheila and I couldn't believe how talented each musician was. Billy took our playing to another level that day. He had us playing in different time signatures, and we were learning from all the musicians he'd brought in. It was so cool to be exposed to jazz fusion and the possibility of new musical directions; it was a special moment to share with my daughter.

When Billy asked me about my plans regarding the Azteca band, I explained that I was still trying to get a new record deal, and that I was having a hard time keeping the band together. He said he could probably get us a deal with Fantasy Records. "But I have an even better idea," he told me. "What about a record deal for you and your daughter? A Pete and Sheila Escovedo album?"

I looked over at my teenage daughter. She was beaming, glowing with the love of music, so happy to be recording with Billy. But then I thought about all the ups and downs Azteca had gone through, Coke's downfall, all the emotional hardship. I didn't want to give up on what was once Coke's dream project, something I'd put so much into.

"I'll think about it," I told Billy. "Thank you so much for the offer."

The decision was a tough one. After much thought, some sleepless nights, and lots of conversations with Juanita,

I came to the realization that this was the new beginning I needed. And it was an important opportunity for my daughter. Azteca had lasted two years, and I still wished we could've gone further. But something new and special–a project with my daughter–was on the horizon. So I didn't have much time for regret.

Billy and I started getting the music together in preparation for recording. He had some original compositions, and I had some that I'd written with Al Bent and Ray Obiedo. Billy suggested a few different musicians, and I hired several of my favorite local ones. It was a great blend of musicians and sounds. We recorded *Solo Two* for Fantasy Records in the fall of 1976.

I still felt some grief over the loss of Azteca, but I tried to stay in the moment, focusing on this new record and the new opportunities for the Pete and Sheila Escovedo band. I couldn't believe I was now recording with my little girl, my first-born, the one that used to sit across from me in her diapers while I practiced, patting her hands as a mirror reflection of my own. Sheila and I began the process of promotion–radio interviews, in-store appearances, and gigs. Billy played a few dates with us and then left town to go on the road with his band. Since Sheila and I had recorded on two of Billy's records by now, our names were getting out there. Since our record sales were good, Fantasy Records suggested a second one.

For *Happy Together*, we used some of the same musicians and several new ones, like the great bassist Randy Jackson (well before his *American Idol* fame). Sheila and I did percussion and vocals again, and Billy and Sheila both played drums. There was a fun spirit of creativity and collaboration in the studio, and we were happy about the final product. The title song, *Happy Together*, is my favorite song on that album.

Despite all our efforts and all the record promotion, we were still struggling to find steady gigs and income. So we accepted whatever other offers we could. Sheila went on the road with someone who'd become a dear family friend, jazz great George Duke, and I kept working locally. The days turned into weeks, and the weeks turned into months. Still, nothing much was happening for Sheila and me. When Sheila turned 21, she decided it was time to move out on her own. She was off to L.A., but mostly she was on the road.

CHAPTER SEVENTEEN

GET OUT OF MY WAY

To make ends meet, I started playing every weekend at Cesar's night club in San Francisco. Times were getting tough again. In the meantime, I started putting another band together with Juan and Peter Michael. They'd really stepped up their playing. I couldn't believe what great players they'd become. Sheila would join us whenever she was back in town. Always a family affair.

To my surprise, Carlos Santana called me from the road one day. He was in Germany, he explained, and was in the process of buying out all of the original Santana members. Instead of keeping it a co-op, he wanted complete control of the music with the option to hire whoever he wanted at any given time. Sheila was out on the road with George, and as hard as it was for me to accept, Azteca was as good as done. So when Carlos asked if I'd join him on tour again, even though I still had dreams of making it on my own, I knew this was an opportunity I couldn't pass up. Plus, I could make some connections to help me with my band in the future.

When I got to Germany, I was in for another wild ride. Carlos warned us, "For some of you guys that haven't been here before, you're going to look out there and see people go crazy. They fight. They fight a lot. It's awful. Don't look out there. Just play and do not look at the audience." We performed on the very spot where Hitler stood on top of a bunker as thousands of his Nazi army troops marched on parade–the same place you see in those haunting clips of him preaching his hatred. The dressing rooms were in the actual bunker–cold rooms, nothing but concrete walls with tiny windows. Carlos warned us again before stepping out onto the stage. "Don't look at the audience." After a few bars of staring down at my hands and looking around at band members, I couldn't help but look out. Carlos was right. It was utter chaos–blood flying, men attacking women, riots. It was all so surreal. I couldn't believe I was standing where Hitler had stood. And there I was, playing music–something so pure, so beautiful, so potentially healing–in this space tainted with one man's evil mission. Images of the concentration camps flashed through my mind as we played *Black Magic Woman*, and the riot grew more and more out of control. This one was so bad that it came out in the papers the next morning. Since coverage of the riot had made it to America, I had to call Juanita to tell her I was okay.

When we got to Milan, the drama continued. We learned that there was a big uproar about our presence. People were complaining that Santana was there to take advantage of the poor since our ticket prices were so high. So the entire band had to attend a televised press conference. We all lined up at a panel outside where we were to play. There was a sea of flashing cameras and journalists. "We're just here to play music," we told them. When we started our show, I felt air rushing past me and soon realized that objects were grazing me. I looked out into the audience and saw the crowd quickly part down the middle. Suddenly, men with ski masks were running toward us, throwing pipes and fire bombs in our direction. Then a Molotov cocktail hit the speaker to my right and exploded into flames. I jumped to my left to avoid the fire. Security came running on stage, throwing blankets over our heads and rushing us down the stairs beneath the coliseum. As we piled into the ambulance, we peeked through the window to see military police attempting to stop the riot. Cars were being turned over, and explosions erupted within the crowd.

We were scheduled to play in Rome the next day, but we were tired and defeated. At the hotel, promoter Bill Graham gave us an earnest pep talk. He was like a football coach in the locker room, trying to inspire a weary team to get its fighting spirit back. "Don't let the Italians scare you! We won't let that happen, right? Let's go to Rome and show 'em what we're made of! You're here to share your music, and that's just what you'll do! So, raise your hand if you're ready to go to Rome. Who's in?" Silence. Not one hand went up. Bill looked down. "And who's ready to go home?" Our hands shot up. So home we went. Bill had given it his best shot. But we were done. Too much unpredictability. Too much violence. Too many mobs and explosions.

Things were getting pretty explosive in the band too. There were too many arguments, and there was just too much competition about who was playing better, and some people were too high to even care. The tour was a whirlwind, and when we got back to the Bay Area, I was glad to be home and to have more financial security than I'd had in a while.

PHOTOS

My parents, Pedro B. Escovedo and Anita Escovedo

My father, Pedro B. Escovedo

Toddler-me in Pittsburg, California

Me in my early teens

Me in my late teens

The Escovedo Brothers: Phil, me, and Coke

My first gig, The Ed Kelly Jazz Band

Chico Ochoa Quartet:
Lalo Reyes, Chico Ochoa, Juanita Puente, Jerry Rubalcaba, and me

The Carlos Federico band at the California Hotel

The Al Zulaica Quartet: Al Zulaica, me, Coke, and Perry Lynn

Juanita Marie Gardere

Wedding day, October 21, 1956

My family at our wedding:
Top row from left: me, Alice, Manuel, and Jay
Bottom row from left: Coke, my mother, and Bobby

Juanita's brothers at our wedding: Joe, Nick Jr., Curtis,
Floyd, and Harold

Azteca days

Juanita and me

The original Azteca

Top row from left: George DiQuattro, Rico Reyes, Flip Nunez, me,
Errol Knowles
Middle row from left: Tom Harrell, Lenny White, Wendy Haas, Victor
Pantoja, Paul Jackson, Bob Ferreira
Bottom row from left: Mel Martin, George Maribus, Coke Escovedo,
Pat O'Hara

AZTECA

© Bruce Steinberg

Azteca, second rendition

Top row from left: Wendy Haas, Victor Pantoja, Terry Bozzio, Bill Courtial, Bob Ferreira, Pat O'Hara, Mel Martin, me

Bottom row from left: Don Grusin, Eddie Henderson, Errol Knowles, Tom Ratley

park-hotel
Karlsruhe

Ettlinger Straße 23
7500 Karlsruhe
Telefon (0721) 60461

Hi Honey,

Sunday Sept. 4, 1977
11:30 p.m.

We just got back from the gig here in Karlsruhe,
Germany. It was outdoors and the weather was cold and
wet. But in spite of all that, there was about 50,000 people.
All of these gigs are starting to look the same.

It was so nice to hear your voice on the phone
last night. I'm sorry if I didn't sound to happy, it's just
that we had been traveling all night after the last gig,
and I was really tired. I think the traveling is what's
making me more tired then the work. I'm finally
getting used to the pace of the set. But when we
have to travel all day + night, that really wears me out.
But I'm glad you called, It makes me realize that your
thinking about the old man, and that you miss me,
just like I miss you.

Well lets see, todays the 4th so theres only
16 more days to go. It seems like the days are
starting to go by a little faster. Oh, some good news!
We just found out today that the next tour, which was
supposed to be 3 wks after I got home, Has been
cancelled. So I'll be home with you all for a while
longer. Honey, I know you don't want me to travel
again, But since Carlos and his people are doing so
much for us, like Helping us with the Hospital, Doctor,
and soforth - I feel that I have to pay them back
for all the money they have given us. And at least
I won't have to worry about where the next check
is comming from. If I can put up with it, I guess
you can too. At least untill we get a little ahead,
or untill Sheila and I can get going. I hope
She understands too. Its not what I really want
and the music isn't what I really want to play, But
I'm just thinking about our future and thats the
real important thing, because I want the Best
for all of us. I owe it to you and the kids
for being so understanding and sticking by me

Sämtliche Geschäftspapiere des Park-Hotel von oserdruck KG - Postfach 1176 - 7590 Achern - Telefon (07841) 21755

On the road in Germany

park-hotel
Karlsruhe

Ettlinger Straße 23
7500 Karlsruhe
Telefon (0721) 60461

all These years, just so I could do what I've wanted to do, so its about time I thought of you this time. The other thing is that if I didn't have this gig, we would be in a lot of trouble with trying to get you well, and I want you to be your old self again, I've been so worried about you, and feeling so bad, because your feeling bad- I want you well + healthy and happy, like you should be- So don't worry Baby, Everything will work out- it always Does with us- You + I are the luckiest people in the world, we have so much, we have eachother, and we have our children, that are so much like us, what more can we ask for- God has given us so much-

Well my love, tomorrow we travel to Essen, Germany, where we'll be for 2 Days, then on to Brussels, Belgium, then on to London Sept. 8- Your Birthday. I hope your Day is filled with Love + Happiness. And I send you all my Love, in this life and any other life, I have but one love, And its only you- we'll celebrate when I get home, so Don't even think that I'm not there for your Birthday.

Well Baby, I have to pack. and get some sleep, because tomorrow we travel again- So I'll close for now, Give my love Zina a big hug + kiss from her Daddy, How I miss her! And to my big Girl Sheila, Tell her I haven't been able to play good without her- And my two sons, Juan + Peto, I miss them Both- And-

All my Love,
All my Life, Always-
To you,
Pete

September 4, 1977, 11:30pm

141

Sheila and me at The Greek Theatre in Berkeley, California

THE ESCOVEDOS

Escovedo family promo shot

Pete Escovedo

Promo shot

Tito Puente and me

Armando Peraza, me, Tito Puente, and Cachao

Me, Angela Davis, and Juan

Dolores Huerta and me

The E. Family: Juan, Sheila, Peter Michael, and me

Sheila, Juanita, me, and Zina

Zina and Juan

Patrice, Juan, Sarah, and Peter Michael

In Performance at the White House: *Fiesta Latina*, with Sheila and the Obama Family

Gallery display of my paintings in Oakland, California (2016)

PAINTINGS

Café de Madrid

Yesterday's Memories

Bird of Paradise

Motherless Child

Maiden Drummer

First Sin

From Harlem to New York

Havana Jam

Rita

Chief Yellow Feather

Self-Portrait

CHAPTER EIGHTEEN

BITTERSWEET

I had a feeling that things with Santana were about to change. Mingo had moved to San Francisco from New York, and he was a better player than me. He was younger too, and hungry. I was enjoying my time at home when I got a call from Santana's management telling me that my services were no longer needed. I had figured that would happen. It was probably noticeable how unhappy I'd been, how fed up I was with being on the road all the time. So, in a way, I was glad to get the notice. I'd been wanting to get back to my own music. But I knew I was going to miss the financial security–the steady paycheck that comes with being in a successful band. I was making a great living just by being a sideman in Carlos' band. And yet, I was unsatisfied. Being a sideman just wasn't for me.

My time playing in Carlos' band was well spent. I was finally able to make a comfortable living as a musician, and I could finally provide for my family the way they deserved. I got to travel the world, play for so many diverse

161

audiences, and share the stage with such talents. But playing in that band, any band for that matter, no matter how great the music, can get complicated. There are so many business dynamics to contend with. There was some unpredictability in terms of management and leadership. Carlos was changing, even going back and forth between being called Carlos and being called Devadip. I was getting restless, bored even. We had to play the same songs exactly as they were recorded, night after night. There wasn't much room to improvise, and I was longing to express my creativity.

Despite my desire to spread my wings, the way it all ended was hard for me. Carlos had been such a good friend–always coming by the house, hanging with us, jamming with us, chatting with Juan and Peter Michael, and bringing flowers to Juanita and Sheila. We hung out on the road a lot, ran together, ate together, and spent hours talking about music and life. So to get the "Thank you but goodbye"-call from his management felt abrupt. Carlos' calls and visits stopped. We lost touch. I felt thrown away and forgotten.

In Sheila's memoir, *The Beat of My Own Drum*, she offers some backstory that I wasn't aware of at the time. It's possible that her relationship with Carlos had an impact on my employment with him, but I didn't know anything about that then. The lack of explanation left me to make up my own conclusions. Mostly, I was hurt.

But time is a blessing, and time does heal. Nowadays, I'm always happy to run into Carlos. We greet each other with a warm embrace. We had the opportunity to play together at the Greek in Los Angeles, and it was wonderful. (It was a benefit concert for Dolores Huerta, a remarkable woman who is family to me.) Carlos and I have occasionally shared the stage for other events as well. He seems more grounded, more at peace, and happier than ever. I'm grateful for the time I had with him, and with perspective, I've realized that friendships can take many shapes and forms. Being a member of Carlos' band helped me to establish my name in the industry. Being on those albums allowed me to be a part of music history. It all worked out for the best. Carlos, *gracias amigo*.

CB80

Since I was no longer with Santana, I was freed up to take more local gigs and smaller tours. In the summer of 1979, I went on the road with Stephen Stills which was a cool four-week run. I went down to Los Angeles for my rehearsals with Stephen, which allowed the kids and me to visit Sheila. George Duke was producing a demo she'd been working on. My brother Bobby came to my first show with Stephen in Visalia since that's where he was living at the time. As usual, Bobby had to get in on the act, so he sat in with the band. Stephen got a kick out of him. Back at the hotel, Bobby continued his one-liners and had the band in stiches.

When we played in San Francisco, I was so happy to see Sheila, Zina, Juan, Peter Michael, and Juanita show up and surprise me. Sheila sat in on drums and, of course, Stephen wanted her to join us for the rest of the tour. She was able to do a lot of the remaining dates which made the humdrum of road life a lot more fun. It also made me much less homesick. We got to hang by the hotel pool, have meals together, sit in with Tito when we were in New York, and experience some unexpected perks like Stephen treating us to ringside seats for the Duran vs. Palomino fight.

Journal entry excerpt: July 2, 1979

Another tour down. Having Sheila there made a big difference. I wonder how many more tours are in my future. Only God knows, and I thank him for this life and for my family. Without them, none of this would be worth anything. I'll be 44 soon. There's so much more to do. More music to play. More places to see. More life to live. What a gift this life is.

CB&O

When I turned 44, I was ready for a new chapter. I'd been ready to record some new material for a long time, so when I got the go-ahead that I could get in the studio, I was excited. I booked some rehearsal time, got the band together, and worked on five new songs for a demo. We did the recording in two days and finished mixing in one day. For one of the songs, a ballad, I decided I should sing with a low voice. So I did that one early in the morning, when my voice is naturally more raspy. I took a shot of Hennessy right before. Ah, the music business, where you can drink hard liquor in your "office" in the morning.

I waited for weeks until finally getting the news that the producer I'd sent the songs to didn't like it. He didn't offer any feedback about why it was a no-go. All that work for nothing. The ups and downs of the business never end. I tried not to let this particular "down" stop me. I never wanted to let someone's opinions thwart my plans.

In the meantime, Juan and Peter Michael were performing in different local gigs. Sheila was on the road with Confunkshun and recording with George Duke down in L.A. I was playing gigs with Coke and relying on my Santana royalties to stay afloat. During my daily runs, I tried to think creatively about what my next move would be. I thought about another demo. I thought about other musical directions. *I just have to keep trying and believing that something good will happen soon,* I'd tell myself as my feet hit the pavement around Lake Merritt. *The best is yet to come.*

About six months later, I got word from the MGM Grand Hotel in Reno that they liked my demo and wanted us to audition. So I rented a bus big enough for the band, family, and friends, and we took a road trip. The band was decked out in black tuxedos while Sheila, Juan, Peter Michael, and I wore all white. We knew we looked good. But apparently our sound wasn't what they wanted. They thought we were "too Latin" to play there. So much for Reno.

Back to square one. Juan and Sheila decided to study music at Laney College while Peter Michael was working with Bill Summers and Confunkshun. I decided to put the family band on hold since Sheila landed a gig with Diana Ross at the Circle Star Theatre and then would be off on tour with Herbie Hancock. I started working with the Latin Rock All Stars, made up of a bunch of guys who used to be in Santana, Malo, and Sapo. Sheila, Juan, Peter Michael, and their friend Paul Green created an award show where they recognized artists like George Duke and Al McKay. They presented me with a Lifetime Achievement Award. I wasn't ready to say that I'd achieved enough for one lifetime, but what a wonderful thing to receive from my kids. Acknowledgement from them is the most rewarding acknowledgement there is.

Later that year, at my niece Sandra's wedding, we all got to spend time with my father and Cleo. It was the first time since I was little that I'd seen my mother and father in the same room. I tried to spend extra time with my mom that day, knowing it must've been hard for her to see him there with his new family. Despite all the rough times, she still loved him. My father seemed so happy as he talked about his children with Cleo. It was great to see his face light up, but I couldn't help but feel some jealousy, wishing he'd been that connected to us when I was young. I guess, like my mom, I had a deep down longing for things to have been different.

Since our lease at Knowland Avenue was up, we found a new spot: 4847 Geranium Place. It had wonderful views of the woods and the city beyond, and it was close to Zina's school. We needed to be near her school since it helped to ensure her emotional safety. She had struggled with anxiety for a long time, and she needed to be near the family. I don't know if it all started when she was very young and in school, or if it started that one Easter Sunday in church when we saw her have her first panic attack. Watching your child have a panic attack, trying to comfort her, trying to make the fear disappear from her mind–it is a helpless experience.

Years earlier, her school called to tell us that we needed to pick her up. She'd been scared of something, they said. They weren't sure what. She'd started crying. *Come get her.* And so we did. The school nurse suggested we take her to a psychologist to be "examined and evaluated." The psychologist explained that she was "an emotional child" and encouraged us to put her in weekly therapy. Eager to do whatever we could to help her, we agreed. But over time, she got worse. We were on a mission to find the right person to help her. We wanted answers, a cure, a strategy. At some point she was given the diagnosis of Panic Disorder with Agoraphobia. Her biggest fear, they told us, was her fear of being afraid–anticipating that another panic attack could come. And the worst fear was of having this kind of attack without a safe person nearby. We were her safe people. So her world got smaller and smaller. She couldn't go to school. She couldn't go far from the neighborhood. Soon enough, she couldn't leave the house. Sometimes she couldn't leave her room.

As she got older, Zina's anxiety continued to plague her. She struggled with fears, heavy emotions, and painful thoughts. Once she even had thoughts about ending her life.

Juanita had to be with her in order for her to do anything or go anywhere. I now know that the two of them kept a lot of Zina's daily struggles from me. I guess they thought it'd be too much for me to handle. It hurt to see her suffering and crying so much. Zina says that her mom was her "second chance at life." Juanita was her strength and her backbone. Women–they're the stronger ones.

Even now, Zina still struggles with anxiety. But she's come so far. Her courage to heal has brought her far outside her comfort zone. She's taken charge, fought for her life, and worked toward peace of mind. And I'm so, so proud of her. She is living proof of the bright light at the end of the dark tunnel.

A "rock bottom" moment for her was when she went off of her anxiety medication. Since she went off suddenly, without tapering, she got incredibly sick. We felt we were losing her. Our dear friend, a practitioner of holistic medicine, Dr. Louie Yu, came to our rescue. He visited Zina every day until she was back to good health. Eventually she decided that some medication would be appropriate, on an as-needed basis. A return to therapy also helped. And then, her participation in Landmark Education courses led her to some wonderful breakthroughs. These classes gave her a new way of living, a new way of viewing her past and her relationship to her anxiety. And now, she has freedom. She has a great job, a great home, and–most important–a great love of life itself. She can venture out on her own and enjoy so many things that before seemed impossible–cruises, flights, walks on the beach, big music festivals, road trips. She's soaking in the simple wonders of every day, knowing how blessed she is to have her life back, and to have a say in how her life will go. She has a mission now–sharing about what she's overcome, and where she's going. One of her Landmark Education courses inspired her to make a short documentary, *Freedom from Four Walls*, to help others with similar struggles. Now her life has new meaning and new purpose. It is a true blessing.

CHAPTER NINETEEN

REBIRTH

The first couple of months of 1981 were about the same as the last couple of months of 1980, and so I had no idea how much would change, personally and professionally, by the end of the year. Juanita was working at Hal Stewart's health store and doing some catering jobs as well. I was still playing regularly at local spots as a special guest and working around the Bay Area with my small band: Frank Martin on keyboards, Joy Julks on bass, Larry Schneider on saxophone, Romey Gueroso on guitar, Jules Rowell and Wayne Wallace on trombone, and Sheila on drums. We played at Siboney's and the Santa Fe Grill in Berkeley, Earl's Solano Club in Albany, Horatio Hornblower in San Mateo, and we finally landed a gig at Keystone Korner where I'd seen Tito play when he was last in town. He'd brought in a small band with Patato on congas, Johnny Rodrigues on bongos, Alfredo De La Fe on violin, Bobby Rodrigues on bass, and Jorge Dalto on piano. As usual, they played their butts off.

After going into the studio to record her demo, Sheila made the big decision to form her own band. She still found time to join Juan and me for a recording session with Herbie Hancock. Herbie is a great guy and a great musician, someone who treats everyone the same. That's always been something that matters a lot to me. I was never a bandleader who cracked a whip. I always wanted everyone to feel they were a part of what I do. They should feel free to explore and express themselves creatively. That's how Herbie was too.

While things were moving along professionally that year, two personal highlights stand out the most: my first two grandchildren. On June 24, my first granddaughter was born, Juan's first child, who he had with Joanne: Zeawnna Escovedo. Juan came up with the name–a combination of Zina's and his own. On September 21, Peter Michael and Karen's daughter, Nicole Escovedo, was born. God is good. The fact that neither Juan nor Peter Michael were married to the mothers of their children kind of bothered me at first. I saw marriage as the right thing, the first thing. But life has its own way of working things out. My sons have the freedom to make their own choices. I can only be there to offer support and advice when they want it.

None of us can predict the future or, when looking back, fully understand why certain things came to pass. With regard to my granddaughter Nicole, tabloids have had a field day speculating about her early years. Sheila has written about her recollection of things in her memoir. Admittedly, I don't know the details here, and at the end of the day, this is Peter Michael's story to tell. I should also acknowledge that Karen, Lionel, Brenda, and of course Nicole each has their own version.

From my perspective, what was so painful was how things changed immediately after the papers were signed, and Lionel and Brenda Richie adopted Nicole. Things literally changed overnight. We were not let into the

Richies' home even though we'd always been welcomed. When we called, we were hung up on. Security guards apologetically told us they'd been instructed to escort us off the property. We were no longer able to see or speak to Nicole. It was devastating. What were they telling Nicole about us? When would we be able to see her and hold her again? Juanita was inconsolable. I was confused and terribly sad. I still am.

I know that Lionel and Brenda loved Nicole very much. I only wish they would've allowed Nicole to stay connected to her biological family as I think cutting all of us out was not in her best interest.

These kinds of family divides are hard enough for children who aren't famous. But she's in the spotlight. I wonder how she's managed to deal with so many people's opinions and stories. I can only imagine what she believed about why her parents agreed to the adoption and why the Escovedo family suddenly wasn't around her. Juanita and I often ask ourselves, what version does she believe? Who was right and who was wrong? What could we have done differently? Does she know the full truth and all the circumstances? What a burden for her. It brings tears to my eyes as I type this.

We want her to understand our feelings as well. We love her so much. She is my granddaughter, and I wish we could be closer. Only time will tell if this is possible. She has a relationship with both Karen and Peter Michael. Those relationships are private and not for me to describe. Juanita and I see Nicole occasionally, and it warms our hearts to see her and to hug her. But those hugs are far too infrequent. Sometimes I think, now that she's married with a family of her own, maybe things will change. She and her family are in our prayers every night. Whenever she's ready, we are here for her.

CR8O

Back to 1981. In October, Juanita and I celebrated our 25th wedding anniversary at St. Anthony's in Oakland. We decided that renewing our vows would be the best celebration we could think of, but this time we got to have our four children with us. Juanita wore her wedding dress and looked more beautiful than ever. Family and friends filled the church and, later, the reception at Frenchy's in Hayward. A lot of musicians performed for us, but the highlight of the evening was the debut of Sheila's new band. A few months later, we got some surprise news about another wedding: Peter Michael had proposed to Patrice. It was nice to know both of my sons were creating families of their own.

The end of 1981 brought another great surprise, a professional one that for once didn't have anything to do with my music. Painting continued to be my favorite escape from the music business. When gigs were slow, or when I had free time in the day before an evening gig, I'd find myself at the canvas, jazz in the background, and brush in hand. It's more than an escape, really. It's a love supreme. Painting carries me into another thought-space, where I lose myself in an intoxicating mixture of color, shape, emotions, and moods.

I'd never thought about exhibiting or selling any of my paintings. My paintings were personal, shared only with family and friends. But one day, while strolling through Oakland's Jack London Square, I entered a gallery to check out the display. I struck up a conversation with the nice woman behind the desk. Mid-conversation she asked, "Wait, are you Pete Escovedo?" I nodded. "Yes, that's me."

We had a nice conversation about music, art, and our shared love of our city of Oakland. When she found out that I painted, she asked me to show her some of my work. "What's your style?" she asked. That was tough to answer. "Sometimes I start with the subject and then the background," I told her. "And I don't mix a lot of colors on the palette. I like to take it right out of the tube and just paint." I explained how music and art felt equally important to me. "They each require my one-hundred percent," I told her. The difference, I explained, is that playing music feels really free and easy. But with painting, I don't truly enjoy it until after I'm done. With music, I'm often performing, trying to entertain an audience. That's one of the main things in my mind while I'm playing in front of a crowd. I try to read them, play to them, and make them happy. Painting is a much more private self-expression. It's just me and the canvas and the paint. I don't need any applause during or after. I'm not trying to inspire or delight anyone. I guess they both come from the same well of creativity, but they express different parts of me. They're both a reflection of who I am and they go hand in hand. Paintbrush and timbale stick.

"I'm excited to see your work," she said.

I couldn't wait to tell Juanita. I was a little nervous about the prospect of being evaluated by someone in the art world, but I knew it would be a good idea to get her opinion. When I came back with some paintings, I was happy to hear that she liked them. She seemed most interested in the faces in the paintings. "They're sort of sad," she remarked. I had to agree. Sometimes I'm surprised by the emotion that comes out. It feels like parts of my past show up in my artwork: some struggles, some suffering, some pain. I've noticed it's harder for me to paint something right in front of me than it is to paint something from my past–whether real or imagined, a truth or an impression.

She asked me to leave some pieces to sell on consignment, and just a few weeks later, they were all sold. Man, I was in seventh heaven. Soon the art gallery proposed an official art show, so we gathered up all my paintings and brought them in. The show ran for a couple of weeks, and 30 paintings, drawings, and ink sketches were sold. I was amazed. I'd never thought I could do anything professional with my artwork. Then again, there was a time when I never thought I'd be a working musician either.

Getting the check was nice, of course, but realizing I'd never see those pieces again left me a little sad. I thought I'd get over that feeling. But to this day, I still have at least a few moments of sadness when parting with my work. You can sell a song you write, but you never lose it; it's yours to listen to again and again. Another artist might even adapt it in a way that makes it better than you could've imagined. But each painting is one of a kind, and unlike a song, which can be played anywhere, a painting exists only where it resides. So selling one is always a bittersweet experience.

CR&O

1981 ended with a New Year's gig in Redwood City, California. A year into the 1980s already. What would this decade bring for me and the Escovedo family? So many unknowns. As the clock struck midnight, I felt a surge of renewed energy and determination to make more of myself in 1982. I wanted to "make it" for Juanita more than anything. She'd sacrificed so much for me, and she was always by my side, picking me up when I was down, encouraging me to keep on keepin' on. Her devotion to Zina was unwavering. I'm not sure how she managed to keep such a beautiful home, take care of me, the kids, and all of our family and friends. I knew I had an angel on earth, and I wanted to give her more.

Meanwhile, Juan and Peter Michael were absorbed in work and their own family lives, and Sheila's star was on the rise. She was increasingly in demand for recording sessions and tours, and her dedication to her music was undeniable. I kept working with her now and again–with the small band at our regular gigs at Larry Blake's, Earl's Solano Club, Frenchy's, Keystone Korner, and Studio 80. The spots were small, but our music was big. Even when sets were over, they sometimes had to remind us to stop playing. My daughter had inherited my love of music, and it was amazing to watch her grow as an artist. Her spirit and smile sometimes seemed too big for those little clubs. She was destined for more, and watching her made my heart full. Sure, her chops were getting better and better each day, but it was the way she and the music merged–the way her spirit was soaring with every beat–that moved me to my core.

CHAPTER TWENTY

THE ISLAND

The next year brought many more ups and downs. One of the bad days was May 5, 1982, when I got the news that Cal Tjader, who'd been in Manila with his band, suffered a heart attack and died. The news rocked me. I realized I'd never again hear him ask what he always asked when he called. "Hello?" I'd say. "Hey Pete," Cal would say. "How's your clave?"

He was a great friend, a great person, and a great musician. Cal was one of the guys Coke and I studied when we were just starting out. We made sure to see him play whenever he was in town. We knew he was one of the first musicians who could take a standard jazz tune and mix it with Latin rhythms. He influenced us a lot in that way. Cal was always nice to us. He'd spot us in the audience and invite us up to play. Maybe that's why I'm always happy to invite fellow musicians up to sit in with me. Cal always made us feel wanted and welcomed, and it was a feeling I wanted to give all fellow musicians who'd come to check me out. Once we were more established, Coke and I performed concerts with Cal and even recorded on two of his albums, *Tjader* and *Agua Dulce*. Phil was on *Agua Dulce* with us. Cal's band was always filled with great musicians: Armando Perraza, Mongo Santamaria, Willie Bobo, Vince Geraldo, Al McKibben, Chombo Silva, The Duran Brothers, Benny Velarde, and many others.

The first time I performed with him was kind of a fluke. His regular drummer couldn't make it, and Louis Kant, his conga player at the time, recommended me since I'd played in Louis' band before. When Cal started calling out the set, I realized I'd been hired not only for timbales, but for the drums as well. One problem: I'd never played drums before in my life. "Hey Cal," I said, after pulling him aside. "I thought I'd just be playing timbales. I've never played drums." He smiled. "Well you're going to play them tonight." Somehow I was able to get through the night, but I must've sounded terrible.

൚൛

It was always hard moving forward after a loss. Day-to-day life was feeling more challenging than usual. The house on Geranium Place, as big and beautiful as it was, was turning out to be a big headache. The rent was sometimes hard to make, and the house was feeling too big for just Juanita, Zina, Sheila, and me. Aside from stress about rent, there just seemed to be a series of bad luck. Sheila's deal with The Whispers didn't pan out. Zina was experiencing lots of anxiety. To top it off, one night we came home to find a window broken and all of our jewelry and other valuables gone. Juanita had tears in her eyes when she realized all our wedding anniversary gifts had been taken. It was just another sign that it was time to get out of there.

So we moved into a townhouse apartment on Willow Street, a few blocks from the beach in Alameda, a small town across the Bay from Oakland. It took us some time to get readjusted to apartment living, but there were some perks. Our neighbors were friendly, and we loved having a pool in the complex. I swam just about every day and started doing daily runs at the beach as well. Since we were across the street from a shopping center, the distance felt safe enough for Zina to venture out and about. She could ride her bike around the neighborhood without any fear, but going to school was still too hard for her. High school was coming up, and we hoped she'd have the courage to attend. The transition would be a big one. The hardest part about the new place was having to go back to being careful about practicing. I'd been spoiled by the Geranium house, nestled high in the Oakland Hills. I could beat on my drums and blast my music as loud as I wanted. I didn't want neighbor complaints in this new place, so I had to go back to practicing quietly and carefully planning each practice session. Being careful and being a musician just don't go together.

Work started picking up again, and the band was sounding better than ever, so I decided it was time to record another album, one with my own money and my own label, Esgo Records. ("Es" was for Escovedo and "go" was for the last name of my investor, Alex Gonzalez.) I called it *The Island*, a tribute to our new hometown of Alameda. There are some great songs on the album, like *True or False* by Ray Obiedo, which I still play in shows today, and *Nahia* by Ray, Sheila, and her friend Connie Davison, which is the song that people seemed to respond to the most when the record came out

It was a happy time, in part because it was the first time my kids and I all recorded together. What a blast. We had as much fun recording and goofing around in Fantasy Studios as we did posing at Alameda Beach for the back cover of the album—me, Juanita, the kids, and our dog, Derf. The front of the album featured me on a timbale-slash-sailboat. It was a cool concept by Bruce Steinberg, who'd also designed the Azteca album covers. Bruce captured the sense of playfulness and optimism surrounding the creation of *The Island*. But the excitement petered out pretty quickly.

We barely scraped up enough money to press the records, print up 500 copies, and pay the band, who did me a favor by accepting little pay. We worked hard to get distribution and radio play. We were out seven days a week, just trying to hustle it up and convince stores to buy it. We scheduled major concert dates to help get the record out too, but it just didn't go anywhere. Since we only had enough money to make 500 albums, they're hard to come by now. I'm always surprised when a fan brings one for me to autograph. Whenever I see that album now, I'm reminded of how my initial high hopes came crashing down. So much effort, time, build-up, and struggle, and then it just kind of fell by the wayside.

All I could do was keep on making music and keep on hoping for a break. Between local gigs (Keystone Korner, Larry Blake's, Lake Merritt Festival, La Peña Cultural Center, Oakland Festival of the Arts, Kabuki Center in San Francisco, Santa Barbara Jazz Festival, Kool Jazz Festival, The Waldorf in San Francisco, and the Bay Meadows Track) and recording, I was enjoying time in our new spot–daily swims at the pool and daily runs at the beach. The family was learning to love this quiet little island of Alameda. Folks who had lived there for a long time never seemed to leave, and I understood why. My granddaughters, Zeawnna and Nicole, had already turned a year old. Time was, as always, flying.

Unfortunately, as time went on, our little place on Willow Street was becoming less and less appropriate for a musical family. Even though I managed to keep my practicing quiet and infrequent, the late-night ins and outs caused too many tenant complaints. Time for the Escovedo clan to move on. We needed a house again, one where the kids and I could do what we did best–make noise. Just before Christmas of 1982, we found a great one: 2915 Santa Clara Avenue in Alameda. Unlike the last place, this one felt like a real home. We invested a little money and a lot of energy into making it as cozy and welcoming as possible. I had an office above the garage, where I could keep my instruments and practice. It was my own little musical refuge. We had two bedrooms, two bathrooms, a nice front room and dining room, and a backyard that was perfect for our new miniature schnauzer, a gift from Coke and Kathy. They'd found him in Lake Tahoe. Or rather, he'd found them when he wandered into their cabin. After trying to find his owner with no luck–no collar or tag and no reports of a missing dog–they brought him home and asked if we could keep him. We Escovedos can't turn down a stray, animal or human. We named him Derf, Fred spelled backwards.

Days and months were flying by. Time waits for no one. I was pushing the album for air play, and we were booking a lot of gigs. I won a BAMMIE at the *BAM Magazine's* annual award show which paid tribute to local musicians. It was an honor to receive the Best Latin Jazz Artist award, particularly because it was the fans who voted. I was being seen as a legitimate musician in the public eye. That felt good. It's funny how as long as I'd been playing, recording, touring, and getting paid to do it all, I still struggled with feeling like a real musician. I guess I still do. I know I can play, but I'm not great. I'm an average player, I think.

The kids were still following in my footsteps. Juan was gigging with me and others while Sheila and Peter Michael went out on the road to play percussion on Marvin Gaye's *Sexual Healing* tour. They had no idea it would be his last tour. We were all in shock to learn he'd been killed by his own father. After Peter Michael and Sheila came home from the Marvin Gaye tour, Sheila took off to tour with Lionel Richie. (This was long before the Richies adopted Nicole.)

I made 48 on July 13, and on my birthday, I set the goal of running my first marathon in December. I chose Hawaii because, well, why not choose a beautiful place to tackle such a big goal? I started training immediately, well aware that it would be a big challenge for my mind and body.

I was determined. No drinking, no bad food. Just clean living and lots of miles. Over time, I got faster and faster. Making 13 miles one day was a huge feat. I was in the best shape of my life.

CHAPTER TWENTY-ONE

SMILE PLEASE

In September of 1983, I got more sad news: yet another friend gone. Willy Bobo passed away from cancer. I'd visited him as often as I could in L.A. once I heard he was sick. It was hard to watch his decline. He only had the energy to play one or two songs at a time. I met Willy when he was really young, that first time he came to California to play with Tito. Mongo was in the band, and Willy was playing bongos. He was a great player, a great singer, and a great overall entertainer with his own style. Willy was always the clown, smiling and cracking jokes. He and Mongo ended up leaving Tito to join Cal Tjader's band in California. One day Willie invited me over to his San Francisco apartment, where he told me that he was going to leave Cal's band to start his own Latin Soul band. He wanted to know if I'd join as the conga player and go back to Los Angeles with him to help get the band going. I was flattered by his invitation but wasn't ready to make the move to L.A. just yet.

Willy's death made me reflect on the roller coaster life of a musician. Three of my four children were following in my footsteps, and sometimes I worried for them. Music was my greatest gift, but my musical career had taken its toll on me. So many good times but so many hard times too—financially, emotionally, physically. Of course I was grateful for all that I had and for God blessing me with family and music. But the disappointments, the rejections, and the unfulfilled expectations really got to me. Still, I'd never trade this life for another.

CBEO

It felt like it was taking forever to establish myself as a solo artist and band leader. In the early eighties, however, despite the internal challenge I may have felt in terms of fully viewing myself in that way, I was receiving more external validation for my efforts. I got the JAMMIE Jazz Musician of the Year award in 1983 and the BAMMIE Latin Musician of the Year award in 1984. This kind of formal acknowledgement always felt good, especially when it's the public voting. But I was never quite sure what to make of a new statue or plaque on the mantle. *Does this mean I've made it? What is making it?*

I'm still not sure how to answer those questions. But I do know the awards felt like indications that I was a long way from sleeping on the kitchen floor in a tiny Oakland apartment, or from sleeping in that long row of orphan cots in Saint Vincent's Home for Boys. Did this mean I'd kept true to that promise I'd given myself, that day on the ferry, the time when my sister Jay had taken Coke and me out for a day trip? Had I made something out of myself? The awards looked wonderful above our fireplace. But was I a success? I just couldn't tell.

I was, however, able to view Sheila's ever increasing success through a much clearer lens. When she came to Oakland during her tour with Lionel Richie, Juanita and I caught the show at the Coliseum. We were so proud to see her share the stage with someone so "big time." Of course, as always, she was fantastic. Lionel was too. It was great to visit with them and to have her home for a few hours, but our time with her was short and sweet since they had to be back in L.A. for more performances that week.

CHAPTER TWENTY-TWO

PEACE AND JOY

While I was meeting some great professional goals, there was a personal goal I had yet to achieve. I'd continued training for my marathon through the fall and winter, running the streets and the beach of Alameda while picturing the finish line in Hawaii. The day had finally arrived. On December 8, 1983, my nephew "Fast Eddie" and friend "3-D" drove me to the airport. I departed from a rainy San Francisco and landed in a humid Oahu. It felt good. I was proud that I'd gotten so physically fit, that I'd set an intention to accomplish something that had once seemed impossible. Even though the marathon hadn't happened yet, the fact that I'd put in all the training and was there in Hawaii about to run my first marathon meant I'd already been successful. I checked into my hotel, which was a block from the beach. Once I got settled in, with my usual routine of neatly putting away clothes, lining up all my hygiene items on a towel, and organizing all my belongings (my kids like to tease me about my rigid unpacking routine), I went out to explore.

When you're a musician, you tend to have at least one friend in whatever city you end up in. I hooked up with my friend Jose Flores who was playing at the Hyatt Hotel a few blocks away. It was great catching up with Jose, and his band sounded great. When I got back to my room, I called Bob Patorian, an old friend from the Azteca days who'd been living in Hawaii since he left San Francisco. We went to a club called TH's where Butch, Charlie, and Ace were playing. Then we went to see Buddy Barnill, another musician from home, play at another spot. I was beyond burnt out when I got back to the hotel and a little worried about getting the rest I'd need for my big run in a few days, so I went straight to bed.

The next morning, Bob and I went over to Butch's for breakfast. We hung out for a while and then went to visit Flip Nunez, another old friend from Azteca. We did a lot of reminiscing and a lot of laughing. Bob and Flip gave me a driving tour of the island before I went back to the hotel to go for a run. My run was interrupted by some rain, so I ended up hanging out with Bob and Flip again. Another late night. I let myself sleep late the next day and then went for a long walk and a swim. It was time to rest. The race was the next morning. I turned in early but was feeling too excited and nervous to sleep. I wondered if I was ready.

When my alarm went off at 4:30 a.m., I wasn't sure if I'd slept at all. I got into a warm shower and did my stretching exercises. My mind was still swirling with thoughts. This run felt like my own personal Super Bowl. It was one of my life's biggest challenges. I'd be relying on just my body and my mind to accomplish this huge goal, and this was the day–26.2 miles in the hot weather of Hawaii. I couldn't stop the worrying. *Will I make it? Will my legs hold up? What if I hit a wall and give up?*

I arrived at the Aloha Towers at 6 a.m. and joined the crowd of 10,000 runners. I'd be in this community of fellow runners, but I'd also be all on my own. A solo act like never before. When the gun went off, there was an eruption of cheers and screams. I started out slow, doing my best to pace myself. If I could finish in four hours, I'd be satisfied. I'd never run more than 14 miles, so if I could get that far, another 12 miles might be possible. At six miles, I felt good, running about ten minutes per mile. We passed Fisherman's Wharf, then ran along Waikiki Beach, and then towards the park. At 13 miles, the lead runners were already on their way back. Watching them return gave me a dose of inspiration. I was halfway there, and I felt pretty strong. When I reached 18 miles, I thought of my family, wishing Juanita and the kids were there to cheer me on. A kind of loneliness set in. At mile 20, my legs started hurting. They felt like rubber. I had to stop and walk a little before returning to my run, and at mile 21, I had to walk again. I was initially disappointed in myself for having to take these walk-breaks, but it felt like I had no choice. I was still very determined to finish. When I got to mile 25, most everyone around me was walking as well. I wanted to be running when I crossed that finish line, so I willed my legs to run again. I ran the last 1.2 miles and crossed the finish line at 4 hours, 39 minutes, and 58 seconds. Mission accomplished. Tears were streaming down my face.

I'd worked so hard to get there, and I'd learned that with effort and discipline, anything can happen. I cooled off on the grass, still breathing heavily, the breeze drying my tears. In that moment, my perspective on everything was clear as day. It's like the lenses through which I viewed my life were newly clean. My music, my family, my life so far–I knew I was blessed beyond measure.

I didn't know if my legs and feet could handle any more walking, so I caught a cab back to the hotel. After calling Juanita, I took a long shower, devoured a big steak with all the fixings, and then drifted into a deep and peaceful sleep. I couldn't wait to get home to my biggest cheerleaders–my family–so I could share all the details with them. Juanita, Juan, Peter Michael, and Zina met me at the gate with open arms. Sheila, still on tour with Lionel, called from Japan to congratulate me, and we all got to sing *Happy Birthday* to her. I couldn't believe my oldest had turned another year older. I wished she was home with us so I could give her a proper birthday hug and kiss.

I stuck with running and joined a gym where I could work out in the morning, run from there to the beach, and then head back for a swim. When I could stick to my routine, my mind, body, and spirt were intact. I managed to run half of the Oakland Marathon which felt good. Running daily with various marathon goals was especially good for my mind when work was slow. The record was at a standstill, and in the back of my mind, I harbored worries about one day not having enough money to survive. Like painting, running helped take my mind off financial stress.

⊰∙⊱

On New Year's Eve, I played at the Hyatt Hotel. I started out 1984 playing some gigs with Coke while also playing with my small band whenever I could. To get ready for the Helsinki Jazz Festival, where we'd be backing up Diane Reeves, I rehearsed at Earl's Solano Club with Marc and Paul van Wageningen and Richard Kermode. The festival featured mostly Latin and Brazilian music and it lasted all day and night. It was great to sit in with Tito and his orchestra. We had a good time catching up–sharing the personal and the professional highs and lows. We'd both had many since our last time seeing each other. After a week in Helsinki, I flew back over the North Pole and was happy to be home again. Experiencing life all over the globe is cool, but being home with family is where it's at.

CHAPTER TWENTY-THREE

ANOTHER STAR

My kids, despite my warnings about how shaky the music biz could be, continued to follow their musical dreams. Sheila, while still performing with Lionel, had signed on with Prince to do a record and video. Juan, Peter Michael, and Zina all had a part in Sheila's *The Glamorous Life* video. They rehearsed and shot the video in Los Angeles. Another Escovedo Family affair. Juanita and I were so proud of them all and very glad that Sheila invited her siblings along for that ride. The single was a smash hit and would one day be her signature song. Peter Michael took Sheila's place in Lionel's band, and Sheila hired Juan to play percussion in hers. Soon they were rehearsing to open for Prince's *Purple Rain* tour.

Juanita and I found ourselves in Los Angeles a lot. Peter Michael was playing with Lionel at the Forum on his birthday, so we drove down to celebrate with him. Then a few weeks later, we were back in L.A. for the premiere of Prince's movie, *Purple Rain*, at Grauman's Chinese Theatre in Hollywood. What a scene. We were proud of all Prince was accomplishing, remembering back to when he was just a kid–Sheila's new friend–jamming at our house and telling us how amazed he was to see a family making music together. I recognized in him that yearning for a close family, and Juanita and I went out of our way to be there for him. Years later, Prince would tell us that we felt like his only family.

Sheila and her band's performance at the *Purple Rain* premiere after-party was fantastic. The crowd went crazy. The next morning, while Juanita and Zina stayed a few extra days with Sheila, I left for my regular weekend gig in Lake Tahoe–playing at my buddy Bob Patoria's new restaurant on the lake at Roberts Beach. It felt like a vacation since I could run in the fresh morning air, play in the afternoon, and hang out in the casinos at night (where the band and I tried not to gamble away all our pay).

The back and forth to Tahoe was starting to take a toll on my training. The gig was fun, but it was hard to avoid the casino night life. So I ended up sleeping in more often than not, which wasn't exactly supporting my plan for a morning run. It was time to hunker down. The San Francisco Marathon was coming up, and I didn't want to miss it. I hadn't put in enough training miles, but I was determined to make the race. My family would be there to cheer me on this time, and I knew their support would be enough to get me through it.

The night before the race, we drove across the Bay Bridge to the city and checked into a hotel. After my shower and stretch routine, I woke up Juanita. "Today's your day, honey," she said with a smile. I started out slowly, pacing myself at an eight-minute mile. At mile 16, I saw Juanita flashing her gorgeous smile. I needed that since my feet and legs were beginning to hurt. By the time I reached mile 20, I had to walk a little. At 22 miles, I almost gave up, but runners who recognized me began to cheer me on. Their support made a big difference. I crossed the finish line at four hours and 10 minutes. Better than my Hawaii time. I set a new goal of under four hours for my next marathon.

The more immediate goal, however, was preparing to be a teacher. I'd been hired to teach percussion at Jazz Camp in Cazadero, a weeklong intensive music camp in the middle of some beautiful redwood trees. It would be my first time teaching professionally, and I was pretty nervous. I knew how to play, but did I know how to teach? I'd never received formal instruction myself, so I didn't really have a frame of reference. I brought Juanita along for moral support. The whole outdoor camping thing was new to me too. I prefer the luxuries of a bed and a warm room. Here, there was a tent which sat on an elevated platform to keep us above all the critters. Not exactly my standard on-the-road quarters, but I decided to view it all as an adventure. I crawled into a sleeping bag each night and stared up at the stars. The first night, Juanita and I stayed up giggling and jumping at every little noise. Us city folk living in a forest. We couldn't believe it. I actually left my "GQ"-wardrobe at home and settled into jeans, tennis shoes, and a sweater. I shared my class with Caroline Brandy, a great percussionist. She was fun to work with, and by the end of the week, we felt really connected to our students.

As we settled into fall, Juanita, Zina, and I held down the home front. Juan and Sheila were still on the road with Sheila's band, and Peter Michael was still on the road with Lionel. We continued to grow close to the Richies and would show up to their shows whenever we could. Zina missed her siblings a lot, but it was also nice for her to have our undivided attention. She got to know one of the dancers on Lionel's tour, Sugar Pop, and eventually he became her boyfriend. We appreciated how much he cared about Zina, and with him by her side, she was more comfortable venturing out of the house without us.

⋘⋙

Sheila was getting a lot of press, and her record was steadily moving up the charts, eventually going gold. Her shows were sold out, she was on the cover of tons of magazines, and her video was on constant MTV rotation. Her partnership with Prince was big news, and soon their professional relationship became romantic. She was head over heels and truly living "The Glamorous Life." We were certainly proud, but it was hard for Juanita and me to see how she was changing. We didn't like watching how she treated people, telling them what to do instead of asking them. Our daughter was becoming someone different, not the girl we'd raised. I tried to talk to her about it, but the pull toward this celebrity life and all of its intoxicating perks was too strong. I was so proud of her talent, her work ethic, and her success, but at the same time, I was concerned about what the fame was doing to her spirit.

She moved to Minneapolis to be closer to Prince and his studio, where they'd write and record all day and night. Those two were some serious workaholics. She recorded more albums and was constantly on tour. She'd always been known as a great percussionist/drummer, but she was now getting international fame as a solo artist, and as Prince's drummer and girlfriend. If he called, she came running. I didn't want her to lose herself, but a parent only has so much influence. Fame and fortune can be a dangerous combination, and if you're not ready for it, you can easily go the wrong way. She was under contract with Prince's management company, and they handled her finances. She didn't read the fine print, and she eventually learned they'd taken a big piece of the pie. It was a painful but important lesson for her. It was one of many humbling experiences that led her to rethink how she'd been treating others, become more grounded, and develop her spirituality. In time, she let go of that celebrity-identity, and her true kind nature was back.

When Sheila played with Prince at the American Music Awards hosted by Lionel, we got to see Sheila, Juan, and Peter Michael all performing on the same stage at the same award show. What a trip. They were a long way from doing their song and dance routines in front of relatives in our Oakland front room–those three bright-eyed kids imitating the Jackson 5, the Osmonds, James Brown, and The Temptations. Now they were bright-eyed adults who still got to sing and dance together. Instead of just getting praise and hugs from their family, they were getting professional acknowledgement from the industry. Juanita and I were out in the audience beaming with pride. Our babies were grown, healthy, and living their passions. We had done something right.

CHAPTER TWENTY-FOUR
YESTERDAY'S MEMORIES, TOMORROW'S DREAMS

Slowly but surely, Juanita and I were adjusting to an empty nest. Even our baby, Zina, was out on her own. Sugar Pop got a gig in Vegas with a show called *Splash*. Zina got a part too—as a Sheila E. lookalike—so she moved to Vegas with Sugar Pop. It was hard for us to see her go, but we were proud of her for making the move. We would visit them often, and they'd come stay with us on their days off. Sheila would be celebrating her birthday in Chicago, so Juanita, Zina, and I surprised her there. Escovedos love a surprise. It was great to see Juan and Sheila perform that night and to be with her on her birthday, especially since it would just be Zina, Juanita, and me home for the holidays.

As usual, I ushered in the new year on stage. When the clock struck midnight, the cheers from the crowd, and even the tone of my own timbales, seemed to fade away. So long to 1984 and so long to my 40s. I'd be turning 50 this year, and that felt like a big deal. Everything felt more significant, each day more important. My kids and their kids were growing older. And, of course, so was I. If you're alive, the one thing you can count on is growing older. So how could I make each day matter? How could I truly make my life as meaningful as possible with whatever time I had left? It wasn't about chasing acknowledgement, money, or the temporary satisfaction of a good review or a certain number of album sales. I wanted to be more conscious in my life—enjoying my beautiful family, celebrating the great days, honoring the sad days. I wanted to just be present to the good, the bad, and the in-between. All of it is a part of my one precious life. So why not show up for it all?

On this particular new year, I decided I didn't want to wait around for things to happen. I wanted to make things happen. So instead of waiting for someone to call me with a record deal offer, it was time to do it myself. I would record my first live album at Oakland's Mills College. Wayne Wallace (trombone) and Ray Obiedo (guitar) wrote the charts. Special guests were Ismael Rodriguez and my kids Sheila, Juan, and Peter Michael. I felt a lot more confident this time around. The band and I had matured in our playing. We were tight. We recorded two nights, with two shows a night, and everyone played so well, which is never a guarantee with a live recording—where you can't rewind and give it another try. What you play is what ends up on the record. The band was perfect. No mistakes. Great dynamics. I think all our friends and family in the audience must've helped us loosen up. It felt like a big party.

The album did well. The reception and airplay it got gave me a sense of the kind of satisfaction and professional progress I'd hoped for when *The Island* was released. *Finally*, I said to myself. *Things are looking up*. Wayne and Ray's writing on that album was an essential component of its sound. Those two musicians have been extremely important influences on my musical direction. Like so many of my band members, they went on to accomplish great things. I think of my orchestra as a kind of college. Once the band members graduate, they're off with their degree, capable of anything, ready to pursue their own musical dreams. It's been one of the most rewarding parts of my career–watching like a proud dean as my band members grow and take on whatever's next for them.

I called the album, which ended up being one of my favorites, *Yesterday's Memories, Tomorrow's Dreams*. The title was my way of summarizing that feeling I had while ringing in my 50th year, that state of musing about how I could view what had passed and how I could approach what was to come. Here's my dedication: "This album was recorded live at Mills College Concert Hall February 16 and 17, 1985. It contains music reminiscent of the old Azteca band and of past performances with my family, Sheila, Juan, and Peter Michael Escovedo. The new music, written by Wayne Wallace and Ray Obiedo, creates the band's future direction and overall sound. I respectfully thank family members and fellow musicians for their talent and the magic that we shared over the years–especially the long nights recording this album. Thank you for yesterday's memories and may we all find peace and happiness in tomorrow's dreams. Dedicated with love and affection to Juanita Marie Gardere Escovedo."

After mixing the tracks at Fantasy Studios in Berkeley, it was time to get busy with promoting and performing. I had to take a brief break when I got the flu, but I was able to recover in time for Juan and Angie's wedding. And to celebrate the big 5-0, we had a fantastic party at the Warehouse Club in Oakland. Too many people showed up, so we had to close the doors–a good problem to have, I suppose.

CHAPTER TWENTY-FIVE
NO BUSINESS LIKE SHOW BUSINESS

It was this 50th birthday celebration that led me to my next venture: business ownership. While teaching again in Cazadero Jazz Camp the next month, I kept thinking back to my birthday party, what a huge crowd there was, and how so many Bay Area folks had shown up to celebrate with the family. I started to wonder if I could draw that kind of crowd on a regular basis. Fans always told me they wished there was more live music in the Bay Area, like the kind my family and I played. So I decided to try and give them what they wanted–a joint with great live music every night.

It was a fantasy that went way back. My old friend Al Larios and I used to talk about the ideal night club, the kind we'd open once we made "the big time." I wasn't sure if "the big time" quite described my status, but I did know that folks enjoyed coming to see me and my kids perform. They even loved hanging out with Juanita, who welcomed everyone with a big smile and hug. My album and Sheila's album, plus her increasing celebrity, would be another draw. The family was developing a solid fan base, and so "big time" or not, this felt like the right time.

I was ready to begin looking for a space of my own. I found a spot on Lakeshore Avenue in Oakland, a successful restaurant, Oscar's. They were looking for someone to take over, so in I walked: Mr. Someone. I ordered my usual, scotch on the rocks, and struck up a conversation with the bartender, who gave me the low-down and introduced me to the owner. He looked like a hitman from *The Godfather*. "I have limited funds," I told him. "But I'm hoping you'll take into consideration how my family has some popularity in the Bay." He nodded and smiled. He actually seemed interested. Or maybe he was just desperate to get rid of the place. Soon we were negotiating terms and conditions. We decided that he would keep the license under his name until I could pay him $250,000 to own the place. I'd take over as a renter, and any remodels would be at my own expense. It was a big gamble on my part, as it would take all the money I had to decorate and remodel. But it was what I'd dreamed of for a long time, and I had to give it a shot.

Remodeling meant first tearing down the fireplace in the middle of the main room. Man, that in and of itself was a tough job. Then we had to redo the bar since it was pretty old. Next we had to put in new flooring, faucets, and countertops. We also had to paint, put in new carpets and upholstery, and get to cleaning. We decorated with some of my paintings, gold records, and photos of musicians and the family. Last but never least, it was time to set the scene for music: a bandstand, new P.A. system, grand piano, and stage lights. Soon the neon blue sign out front, "Escovedo's," lit up Lakeshore Avenue.

It was a family affair as usual—lots of close friends and relatives working for the club. We hired bartenders, waiters, and security. My brother Bobby came on as bar manager and Angie's mom, Jacqui, generously lent me some money to cover extra expenses since by now I was cleaned out. Without her, I wouldn't have had any money to actually open the bar. Like, no money for the cash registers the first night. We got a lot of publicity in the papers and radio for the grand opening, October 11 and 12, 1985. We spread it over two nights since the capacity was only 275, and we knew it would be packed. It seemed liked the whole Bay Area showed up. There was a long line around the corner each night, and we had to turn folks away because we'd reached capacity. My band played the first three weekends. Mondays were big band jazz, Tuesdays we had The Ed Kelly Jazz Trio, and Wednesdays were salsa nights. On Thursdays, we featured different local bands, like Ray Obiedo's Rhythmus 21, Voz De Samba, Brenda Vaughn, Freaky Executives, and Linda Tillery. I started bringing in big names on the weekends like Tuck and Patti, Poncho Sanchez, Flora and Airto, Paquito De Rivera, Mongo Santamaria, Tito Puente, and of course Sheila, whose shows were always sold out.

Business was booming. I would've liked to have been there more to keep my eye on things, but I was gigging a lot at the time, so I had to trust those I'd put in charge.

CHAPTER TWENTY-SIX

THE OTHER HALF OF ME

Since things were going well on all fronts, we decided to make my 51st birthday a family vacation. We decided on Las Vegas, where we could celebrate big, catch some shows, and relax. Sheila, Juan, Angie, Jacqui, Peter Michael, Patrice, Juanita, Zina, and I had a special dinner party at one of the casinos owned by Steve Wynn, who was kind enough to let us use a private room. We were having a great time–eating, laughing, throwing around fun ideas about what to do after dinner–when I was told I had an urgent phone call. It was my sister Jay, telling me Coke was in the emergency room in Los Angeles. "He's in critical condition," she said. She and my mother were flying down to be with him.

Coke's health concerns were nothing new, but something in Jay's voice made me think that this time was different. A few hours later, I learned that my intuition was right. My little brother Coke passed away. I wish he could've managed the ups and downs of the music business better. There are so many aspects that feel out of the artist's control, even for the people that make it big. Financially you might make it, but then what happens to your ideas? This one record might sell, and then the other one doesn't. You've got to be strong-minded. When the business challenges got to be too much for Coke, he coped in unhealthy ways. Drugs and alcohol were his escape.

I slowly let it sink in that all of our efforts to get him sober had failed. He would be sick again and again, bleeding internally, in and out of the hospital. I'd plead with him to get well, to take care of himself, to get sober. He'd get back on his feet, seem healthy again, and then go back to the wrong things. Then he'd be sick again, in pain and agony. It was an awful cycle for him and for those of us who loved him. I felt as helpless as I'd been back at Saint Vincent's, hearing his cries at bedtime through the walls but unable to reach him, unable to protect him. He was 45 years young when his body gave up. July 13, 1986. Coke died on my birthday. I felt like it was his way of saying, "You're never going to forget me, big brother." My birthdays would never be the same.

We paid tribute to Coke at the club, dedicating the music to him. All I could think about were our times together. I thought about those two little boys living in tiny places, hoping for more. He was my little brother, the one who I shared so much of my childhood with, the one I looked after, the one who followed me around. He followed my interest in music and soon become a much better musician than me. I thought about the Azteca band voting Coke out because of all the drug use and money lost. There was only one vote to keep him in: mine. It was his dream to start this band, and it was created out of a pure love for music. I wondered what would've happened if the band had managed to stay together. It's a thought that still crosses my mind sometimes. We were just scratching the surface of what could've been, musically. Azteca had a slow build and then a dramatic ending. And now the drugs that had stolen my little brother's mind and body for too long had finally stolen his life.

Memories flooded me–our childhood, Saint Vincent's, all of our jam sessions, and all of those stages we shared. Our days with Carlos Federico, Chico Ochoa, The Duran Brothers, Cal Tjader, The Escovedo Brothers, Willy Colon, the Latin jazz sextet with Mel Martin and Al Bent, Santana, and our dream band, Azteca.

Then I suddenly thought back to that time he cried because he could see I was drowning. His little face, so helpless, so panicked. I wanted to get out of that water as much to comfort him as to keep myself alive. And I did. Once I made it out of that river, I could reassure him that I was fine. I also flashed back to that day I got that scar over my left eye. I can't remember what year it was or where we were living. I know my mom and dad were still together because they both picked me up from the hospital. A bunch of us kids had gone to Mosswood Park, where we ran around playing "Follow the Leader." I'd been closely following a kid called "Fat Sammy" when all of a sudden he came rolling down the hill and hit me hard. I went flying head first into the creek. I couldn't see anything except for the color red in front of my eyes. I literally "saw red." I heard the other kids crying and later learned they thought I'd lost my eye. Coke's cries were the loudest. I wanted to leap up and tell him I'd be fine, but I was too stunned to talk. I got rushed to Highland Hospital to be stitched up. "You're lucky that the injury just missed your eye," a stern-looking doctor said as he leaned over me, shining a bright light in my face.

"What were you thinking?" my mom asked, her expression a combination of anger and worry.

My dad didn't seem mad at all. He was smiling. "I'm proud of you," he said.

I looked up at him. "Why?"

"Because you didn't cry."

"Well, I didn't want Coke to see me cry."

It was a decision I'd made long ago: It was more important to stop Coke's tears than to show any tears of my own. When "Fat Sammy" hurt my eye, it was Coke who was crying. I wiped his tears at Saint Vincent's Home for Boys as our mom drove away and each time a visiting relative had to leave. And, through the years, I did my very best to keep attending to his pain–pain that was sometimes disguised as self-destructive behavior. He wasn't crying at those time, but his hurt was evident. He seemed to need my help, and I did my best to give it. Now he was gone, and there was nothing I could do to protect him anymore. Now I was the one crying.

And so the beat goes on. The music lives on through our children and our children's children. Sometimes it feels like one infinite song, the melody and rhythm passed down from one generation to the next. Harmony. A chorus. A never-ending jam session. Rest in peace, little brother, Joseph Thomas "Coke" Escovedo. Until we play again.

CHAPTER TWENTY-SEVEN

WHATCHA GONNA DO

I found myself craving alone-time to try and cope with the loss of Coke, but the business was requiring more and more of my attention. It was increasingly stressful, and things were taking a turn–a left turn. Some of the people I'd put in charge weren't proving to be all that reliable, and we came to find out that some of the employees were straight up ripping me off. Meanwhile, I was being handed bills for everything. Then the guy who rented the kitchen took his pots and pans and took a hike. I was left with more rent to pay, more bills to deal with, more people to fire, more people to hire, and I was still nowhere near having the cash I needed to buy the club. The ship was sinking and I, its captain, was going down with it. As 1986 came to a close, so did Escovedo's club. Farewell to my dream of owning a successful club. It was hard to let in the disappointment and the sense of failure, and I couldn't imagine ever finding the energy to try it again. It was like losing a home, a place I'd carefully decorated, a place where my friends and family could gather, a place that felt like a part of me. "Well, I guess all the after-parties are gonna have to be at our house again," I told Juanita. She gave me one of her world-class hugs and reassured me. "Things will work out, Honey."

Back to my day (night) job. I started taking gigs anywhere and everywhere to rebuild my savings since the club venture had almost drained me. I stopped journaling for a long while because I felt like there just wasn't much to say. Things felt dim and hopeless, so why record that in writing? I started running again, which probably saved me from total depression. Running got me thinking positively again. "The club's failure doesn't mean I'm a failure," I'd say to myself again and again as my feet pounded the Oakland pavement during sunset runs. Eventually, I believed it.

I continued with performing and recording sessions. A highlight session that year was with Woody Herman for his album *Woody's Goldstar*. Woody's bus (all the big bands traveled by bus back then) pulled up to the studio, and he walked out slowly. I learned he was ill and that a doctor was traveling with him. He had to take a lot of breaks during the session to gather his strength and energy. Even though he was sick, he played like a pro. We recorded live, so I had to pay close attention during rehearsals. Big bands are used to reading the charts a few times, and when that red studio light comes on, they record. Poncho Sanchez, who played congas on the record, was nervous like me. But we got through it and it turned out great. Woody thanked us and then got back on the bus to his next gig. I regret not talking to him more, not finding out more about his life and his inspirations. I have so much to learn, and I wish I'd had more time to learn from him. I didn't know that would be Woody's last album; he would die later that year.

CREW

This was also the year I lost the one who gave me life, my mother. She was 76 when she had a massive stroke and was put on life support. It was so awful seeing her hooked up to those machines day after day. Even though she was technically alive, her spirt was gone. The family got together, and after learning from the doctor that if she ever recovered she would have no brain function, we elected to let her go.

When she took her last breath, her death felt more final than any other loved one's. I found myself thinking about the quality of her life. It seemed like she'd had nothing but hardship from day one. She had a rough marriage with my father. Even after their divorce, her relationship with him seemed to haunt her. She struggled financially, and she had to be apart from some of her kids for much too long. What was it like to leave Alice and Bobby in Mexico with her parents? And what was it like to leave Coke and me at the group home? As painful as that was for me, I never blamed her. I understood that she had struggled alone, trying to feed and clothe and shelter her kids with a waitress' salary. In that tiny apartment with no bathroom, the one where Coke and I slept in the kitchen on a cot, she must've decided that she had no other choice.

She did find love with another man, Jim, a merchant seaman, but their relationship seemed less than ideal. He'd be gone at sea for two to three months, and then would return for a few lovey-dovey days before the arguments would ensue.

I suppose her challenges with marriage and with keeping our family together are what led me to want to create a solid family, to choose Juanita, and to stay in our marriage and focus on family above all else. During the days after my mother died, I couldn't help but feel sorrow about not only my loss, but about her losses–all she missed out on. I took some comfort in remembering the things that did bring her joy. Her grandchildren brought her many smiles, and her wild sense of humor brought her many laughs. While she might not have said it, I could sense that she was proud of me—of my foray into music and of the loving family I'd created.

છઠ્ઠ

As always, the only way I knew to move forward was to focus on work. When I received a call to go on tour with Anita Baker, I was conflicted. I was flattered that Anita had requested me, but I didn't want to go back to being the sideman again. I'd been there, done that; it felt like some kind of slide backwards. I'd spent four years out with Santana, so I knew I could handle just one tour. Plus, I was still stressed about finances. I needed the steady pay check.

In mid-July, we started rehearsals for the *Rapture* tour in L.A. Bobby Lyle, a very nice guy and great piano player, was the musical director. Anita didn't come to rehearsals until the band had nailed down all the songs. She greeted me with a warm smile and open arms. She was kind as can be and such a talented vocalist and songwriter. Soon we were off: Hawaii, Cincinnati, Detroit, Boston, New Jersey, Saratoga Springs, Cleveland, Chicago, Milwaukee, Minneapolis, Ohio, New York, Maryland, and Atlantic City. I took it upon myself to set an example for the young musicians in the band. When her direct feedback to them or the sound engineers seemed tough, I tried to help them see it as life training. Some artists are incredibly particular about every single detail. Intricacies of solid musicianship are important, and sometimes an artist is committed to complete excellence. Their delivery might not always be the way you want it, but that's why I think it's helpful to just think about their overall intention—a great show, the best possible sound, and giving the audience something wonderful. The tour ended in Sacramento on September 18, 1987. I got close to Anita and the band (including

Gerald Albright and the Perri Sisters) and really enjoyed my time on the road with all of them.

ভ৪৯

Back from tour, I was ready to work on my own thing, but I wasn't sure what direction to take. In December, Tito and his band were recording in San Francisco for Concord Picante Records. I went by the studio to hang out and ended up having a conversation with Carl Jefferson, who owned the record company. He was a big jazz fan. Every year, he'd put on a summer jazz festival in Concord, California, and eventually he started Concord Records. His roster was an amazing who's-who of jazz greats: Charlie Byrd, Flora and Airto, Cal Tjader, Mongo Santamaria, Tito, and many others.

"What are you up to lately?" he asked me.

"Just trying to push my own record and company, but it's not going too good," I admitted.

"Come into my office next week," he said. "Let's talk more. Bring your record."

After listening to my latest record and telling me he liked it, he said he'd call me in a few days with some ideas. Those next few days felt especially long. I had no idea what, if anything, this would lead to. As promised, he called and invited me back to his office, this time with an offer to put the record on his label, distribute it, and pay me for the amount I spent making it. "If all goes well, we'll do another one." My partner, Alex, and I jumped at the offer. Just like that, my record was re-released on Crossover Records. I felt a renewed appreciation for the quality of the last record, *Yesterday's Memories, Tomorrow's Dreams*, as it's essentially what got me to this next important step.

By early 1988, I was indeed offered to sign with Concord and record another one. It would be called *Mister E*. I was eager to get into the studio since I felt the band and I had gotten a lot better, and we had some great songs to share. The recording process was surprisingly smooth and easy, and the musicians did an incredible job.

What didn't go that smooth and easy, however, was my plan for a new image to accompany the new record. For the cover of the album, I wore a smoking jacket and posed in a big chair in front of a fireplace in San Francisco's Whittier Mansion. I was going for that cool, laid-back, Hugh Hefner vibe. Right before the photo shoot, Juanita insisted that I dye my salt-and-pepper hair. "You should dye it black, honey," she told me. "That'll give you a younger look for the album and tour." I didn't want to, and the record company didn't want me to either. "Your grey hair is iconic," they told me. "It's part of your signature look. And it fits the distinguished appearance we want for the cover." But it ain't easy to say "no" to my wife when she's set on an idea. So I let her dye my hair over our kitchen sink. At first it looked okay, and when we shot the cover, the color was still hangin' in there. But in a few weeks, when the black started fading, all kinds of orange, yellow, brown, and red took its place. Man, I looked like some kind of unintentional punk rocker with a head full of tropical flowers. I had to wear a big felt hat every day for months.

Despite the hair-drama, the *Mister E* promotion, gigs, and radio-play all went great. I dedicated the album to my brother Coke: "His spirit, love, and inspiration will forever live within me." It was nominated for a GRAMMY, an honor I'd been dreaming of for years. (I'm still dreaming of a win, though.)

I spent the rest of the year performing all over the place, trying, as always, to promote, promote, promote. We took a few breaks here and there so that Juanita and I could travel to Europe to visit Juan and Sheila on tour. Spending time with my wife, sightseeing, and visiting our talented kids made all the stress from the club closing seem light years away. Sheila took us to Miami for a short vacation. We had a blast swimming, sailing, fine dining, and sunbathing. We sure know how to enjoy ourselves and each other.

We don't take these trips for granted or this kind of time together. We never forget those days of careful budgeting, when Juanita and I would sneak the kids into drive-ins because we couldn't afford to pay for each of them, or when "family vacations" meant staying one day at a cheap motel in some hot inland city just so the kids could get a day at a pool.

I stayed busy with gigs, an appearance with the family in the film *Ford Fairlane*, TV performances like *The Arsenio Hall Show*, and recording sessions like the one Juan and I did with Barry White. And right after my 54th birthday, I was back to Cazadero Jazz Camp, though this time as the musical director. There was also a lot of international travel, like my trips to Japan–Tokyo, Osaka, and Fukioka. Japan has always been one of my favorite places to play. I love how the venue staff will line up and clap as we enter and exit the stage. It's a gracious formality. The Japanese are an amazing audience. They're appreciative of American music, and they're big fans of Latin jazz. After the show, they have us sign incredible pieces of memorabilia–magazines we were featured in decades ago, albums we played on that you can't buy anymore, and photographs I don't even remember posing for. I was inspired to infuse my music with Japanese culture. (Later, I would even record the song *Like a Volcano*, written by Japanese pianist Naoya Matsuoka.)

೧೫೨೦

After a performance in Aruba, I flew home to prepare for a series of shows billed as *The Percussion Show Down* with Tito Puente, Sheila, Juan, and Peter Michael: June 21 in Sacramento, June 22 San Diego, June 23 in Bakersfield, and June 24 in San Jose. It was always great to perform with Tito and the kids, but we had one major problem: Nobody showed up. We blamed poor promotions. We had friends who lived down the street from the venue telling us they didn't even know about it. The investors put all their money down on these huge arenas and theatres so there was no money left over for advertising. And there wasn't much money to pay us either. We couldn't draw flies. What a disaster. I think we still hold the record for the least amount of audience members at the Sacramento arena. When we walked out onto that stage for the first show, we saw more employees than paying customers. Tito kept us in great spirits though. "We still get to play together," he said. "Let's have fun!" We asked Tito if he wanted to cancel the remaining dates, but he chose to stick with it. He was having a ball with us backstage and on stage, and it didn't matter to him if there were ten or ten-thousand people watching us play.

The "tour bus" they provided looked more like one of those old buses in Mexico where they put the chickens and goats. When that jacked up bus pulled up, covered in different faded colors, I thought it was a prank. It was like the Partridge Family 2.0., only not as groovy. "You've gotta be kidding," I said. There was no air conditioning, no television, no beds, and no radio. I promptly called a friend for a more comfortable ride.

I was looking forward to seeing Tito again in August, when he'd be receiving his star on the Hollywood Walk of Fame. Those plans were instantly derailed when Sheila had to be rushed to the hospital because of a collapsed lung. She'd been working so hard for so long, and it had caught up with her. Tito and Margie came to visit her at the hospital, and we all just sat by her and prayed. We stayed until she was finally released. It took her a while to get back on her feet, but with the help of a lot of great doctors, she was eventually able to feel healthy and back to normal again. Thank God.

Work stayed pretty steady for the remainder of the year. I did some gigs with Larry Vucavich, a jazz piano player from Europe who was living in San Francisco. Playing with his trio was kind of a cool change of pace. The next few years, I played a lot of dates around the Bay Area, the U.S., and Japan. Interest in my record had begun to die out, and Concord didn't pick up my option to record another. So I went searching for a new label. I'd met the president of Motown's jazz label, MoJazz, when he was a young concert promoter, and he offered me a deal once we reconnected. But first I had to record two Christmas songs with some other artists for the MoJazz Christmas album featuring Norman Brown, Eric Reed, J. Spencer, Wayne Johnson, Terra Sul, and myself. The timing wasn't great for me. Before I could record my album, the company shut down. It just couldn't get off the ground. "When one door closes, another one opens," I tried to tell myself.

While waiting for that other door to open, I kept doing dates with my band. Juan had put a small band together to perform in Japan for three months, so I had to find someone to replace him temporarily. I didn't like that he'd be away from home for so long, and it's never as fun playing in the band without him, but I was proud of him for doing what he'd been wanting to do–something of his own. Sheila and Peter Michael got to visit him during a stop on their tour with Sheila's other band, The E Train. Crazy to think that those three siblings who used to meet up at Casper's for hot dogs in Oakland were now meeting up at jazz clubs for sushi in Gifu.

CS&O

The work kept coming for all of us, and I assumed it would stay that way. But in January of 1995, I learned not to assume anything. I started having sharp pains on the left side of my body. The pain got worse and worse each day, so I called our doctor who sent me straight to the hospital. They ran a series of tests but couldn't figure out what was going on. They were giving me shots of morphine every hour to ease the pain. I couldn't eat or sleep, let alone walk to the bathroom. Finally they figured it out: I had shingles. Those days in the hospital felt like the end of my life. I'd never been so sick, so helpless, so at the mercy of my physical limitations.

There was too much time to think. My mind was swirling with negative thoughts. *Will I play again? Will I ever get my health back? Why on earth have I ever taken my health for granted? Is this it for me?*

After two weeks, the doctors said I was on the mend, and I was cleared to go home. What a relief. After a few more weeks of rest and Juanita's TLC, I was able to feel a little more like myself. But I'd lost a lot of weight and felt weak. Still, I wanted to keep my commitment to doing the drum clinic in Sacramento I'd scheduled awhile back for Toca, the percussion company I endorse for my timbales, congas, and hardware. Toca had always been so supportive. I didn't want to break my word or let down the students, so I showed up and did my best. But I had to stop halfway through because I just didn't have the energy or strength to do my demonstrations or engage in any kind of productive Q&A. I felt terrible about giving them only half of the clinic, but it was one of those moments when I had to remind myself I was human. I tell my kids to slow down, to rest up, and to take care of their physical health while pursuing this crazy music-life filled with jet lag, interrupted sleep, and nonstop hours of go-go-go. It was time to heed my own advice.

By the next week, I was back to my old self, eating and sleeping normally, and playing music the way I used to. The show must go on, and soon I was back on the road. I did a short tour: Albuquerque, New Mexico, and Denver, Colorado. I haven't taken my health for granted since then. We are blessed to wake up each morning, to breathe, to have whatever strength and physical abilities we have.

My recovery happened just in time for me to get a call from Japan asking me to join Naoya Matsuoka for dates at the Blue Note clubs in Tokyo, Osaka, and Okinawa. I brought along my friend Henry Royal to help with travel and business arrangements. I knew Naoya was good but was surprised to find out just how well the band played Latin jazz. Naoya told me he'd been a student of Cuban music, which was clear from his compositions. We had a great time playing together, and it was an especially good international trip for me since I'd so recently found gratitude for life itself. I made sure to appreciate every single blessing during that trip–surprising cultural similarities and differences, friendly club staff, excited audience members, kind strangers, and the exquisite connection I felt on stage playing Latin music with Japanese musicians. I was learning that life was full of all kinds of wonders, especially when I chose to look for them.

Meanwhile, my kids were staying busy. Zina grew tired of the Vegas night life, and her relationship with Sugar Pop came to an end. She came home to Alameda and then joined Sheila on a bus tour around the states. That's when she got close to Scotty, Sheila's sound engineer. In time, they became much more than friends. Scotty had to go home to Minneapolis when the tour was over, but he'd visit Zina in Alameda whenever he could. Since the long-distance thing was hard for them, they decided to give their relationship a chance by living together. She still had her fears, but she was more and more in control of them. It was hard to see her go again, but we wanted her to feel as confident and independent as she could out there in the world. We were proud to see her taking this next step.

Juan, Sheila, and Peter Michael were on the go too. Juan had returned from Japan, and the calls from other artists were coming in nonstop. He went out on tour with Terry Lynn Carrington, Lou Vega, MC Hammer, and Patti LaBelle, while Sheila and Peter Michael were still out touring with the E. Train. Juanita and I were missing the heck out of our kids, but we were comforted by visits with our grandchildren.

CR80

I wondered what would be next for me musically, and before the end of my 60th year, I got an answer. Concord Records called asking if I'd do another record and a new deal.

Cool, I was ready and able. It had been nine years since I recorded my last one, so it was way past time. Since it had been so long, I knew I had to come back with a bang. I was determined to make this one better than the last, with at least one song that was good for radio. Without that, it was hard to get the word out. So I decided to use a lot of Smooth Jazz musicians and to cover a song that could get a lot of radio play. I chose a beautiful ballad by family friend El DeBarge, *All this Love*. Later, El told us that my cover was his favorite rendition of the song. That meant a lot.

Since we were thinking about moving down to Los Angeles–a big decision as Oakland felt like our forever-home–I called this record *Flying South*. That possible move was weighing heavy on my mind, and so it felt like the right title. I liked the theme of flying and integrated that into my painting for the record cover: a bird flying over the percussion. This time around, I used many past collaborators as well as some new ones, like Gerald Albright on saxophone and Lalah Hathaway on vocals. I co-produced this record with Peter Michael, which was a lot of fun. I was so impressed by his growing talent as a producer. I dedicated the record to the memory of my mother, Anita Valenzuela Escovedo. It was still hard to believe she was gone.

CHAPTER TWENTY-EIGHT

MISTER E.'S

Flying South was doing well, though it didn't get the GRAMMY nomination I'd hoped it would. (A GRAMMY is still a big "bucket list"-item for me.) With all the attention from the record, the band was working a lot, and I was getting invitations to participate in lots of special events and projects like the film *Jack*. I managed to put away some money for a rainy day. And man, was it about to thunder and pour. I thought my dream of being a club owner had died for good, but yet another big surprise was coming my way. My nephew Rene called to invite me to see him perform at a club in Berkeley. He mentioned that the owners were tired of running the place and were looking for someone to take over. This place was run solely as a night club. No restaurant to deal with, so I was immediately intrigued. When I walked up, I felt a rush of energy. It was on Shattuck Avenue in the heart of Berkeley, not far from UC Berkeley and Telegraph Avenue, near lots of public transportation, restaurants, stores, hotels, and movie theatres. I walked down the wide staircase to the club, which reminded me of one of those 1920s speakeasies down below the entrance floor, and as soon as I walked in, I began to imagine what it could look like if I took over.

The club was family-owned, and we decided I'd take over the club as a manager in order to use their liquor license. To the general public, I would be seen as the new owner. My goal was to create a first-class jazz club. Once we agreed on terms, the next step was to remodel with the Escovedo touch. Once again, I went all out. There were three bars that needed to be redone and partition walls to remove. New carpets, new hardwood floors for dancing, new chairs, bar stools, tables, paint, restroom renovation, P.A. system installation, and a stage and dressing room for the artists. I decorated with my paintings, some gold records, various music memorabilia, and some half-shell congas and bongos created for me by Toca. I spared no expense. Mister E's would be the dream club that would last because I'd learned my lessons from the last club.

We had our grand opening on November 11, 1997, with a reception hosted by the mayor of Berkeley which was covered by all the press outlets. Sheila, Juan, and Peter Michael joined my orchestra on stage. It was jam-packed. This time, running a club was a lot more fun. The space made more sense, and I had more experience booking acts. I brought in a wide variety of musicians and performers, from jazz, to R&B, to salsa, to big band. The crowds were pretty steady, and things were looking good financially. Zina did a great job managing things, and Juanita was a natural hostess. Nobody can make someone feel more welcome than my wife can. I got just as much positive feedback about her warm greetings as I did about the layout and music! My manager, Victor Pamiroyan, handled all the bookings with professionalism and integrity. We were staying afloat and even able to start saving. Slow nights were a little stressful, but we kept bouncing back and could consistently make rent, payroll, liquor bills, and band fees. There was no end in sight.

The kids and I kept busy making music. Sheila and Peter Michael were off to L.A. to play in the house band on Magic Johnson's late night talk show, *The Magic Hour*. I was so proud that Sheila was the first ever female musical director for a talk show. Peter Michael was later hired as musical director for the *Martin Short Show*, and after that the *Wayne Brady Show*. Juan was busy recording with various artists, and when he was available, he joined my band in our various gigs around the U.S., including, of course, the Bay.

And when I wasn't on the road or at the club, I was hard at work on my next Concord Records project, *E Street*, recorded at Fantasy Studios in Berkeley. I created the cover art for this one as well, where "E Street" represents the road I'd traveled in my musical life. I added some of the clubs I'd played as well as Court Street Church in Alameda where we went on Sundays. For me, the most special song on that album is *Lord Remember Me*, featuring Vallejo's Revival Center Ministries Choir. It's the first time I ever did an overtly religious song on a record. I had to fight hard to get a religious song on a Latin jazz CD, but I stuck to my guns and convinced Concord to take the risk. I'm also really fond of *Like a Volcano*, the one written by that great Japanese pianist, Naoya Matsuoka, who I'd so enjoyed working with in Japan. For this record, I brought in a lot of the usual personnel and a few special guests. It was a large project which meant lots of contributors.

When the record came out, the city of Emeryville paid tribute to me by naming an actual street, E Street, after me. At the ceremony, I stood in awe. There I was, in the same city where my struggling single mother spent summers working at the Del Monte Cannery, and I just couldn't believe they'd named a street after me here, in the East Bay–the place I always called home, the place that had in many ways raised me with its culture, its people, its music. Despite how great the record turned out, it didn't get much radio play. But I got a lot of satisfaction in hearing from fans that it was one of their favorites. Ultimately, that's what matters more.

CHAPTER TWENTY-NINE

TAKE SOME TIME

For me, the year 2000 will forever be marked by significant loss. The first loss was the death of one of my dearest friends. In May, after hearing that Tito Puente was feeling ill during his last performance, I called him at his home in New York. He let me know he was feeling okay, but that he had a simple operation scheduled to remove some blockage in his heart. "I'll be back on the scene in a few days, Pete." He wasn't worried, and so neither was I. "Okay, Tito. I'll check on you in a few days."

Tito died during his operation, but I didn't believe it. We'd just spoken the day before, and suddenly he was gone. It was like losing Coke all over again. I traveled alone to New York for his funeral. The funeral home was mobbed like it was a sold-out gig–so many people in the building and standing in lines around the corner, despite the rain, wanting to pay their respects. It was too packed for me to get inside. Not getting inside contributed to my denial. If I couldn't see the coffin, then maybe he wasn't in it. A few friends spotted me, and we joined the procession to the burial site. There was a church service there, and some of Tito's friends and family gave tributes honoring who he was as a musician, husband, and father. I tried to make my way over to Margie and the kids, but they were surrounded by too many people. I walked over to the gravesite and gave myself a moment to try and accept the fact that it was designated for Tito. I couldn't go to the final burial site. I just couldn't watch the coffin, containing my friend's body, being lowered into the earth. I got a ride back to my hotel and flew back to Oakland the next morning. I called Margie to let her know I'd been there and to hear how she and the kids were dealing with his sudden passing. I couldn't imagine their shock since it still didn't feel real to me, though I'd just been across the country, standing at his gravesite.

Tito was by far the most important person, musician, mentor, and friend in my musical life. I was grateful we'd had so much time together, and that some of our music could be preserved for the ages–like his participation in *E Music* and the live record/DVD we did with Sheila called *Latina Familia*. I thought back to how powerfully he influenced me. There was one of Tito's songs, *Mirame Mas*, that Santos Colon sang, and that I later played in our band. Whenever I could make it to his show, Tito would always call me up to sing that song. Tito and I wrote a song together, *Ah Ha*, that was on Azteca's first record, and we recorded again as part of *The E Medley* on *Yesterday's Memories, Tomorrow's Dreams*. He also played on *E Street Mambo*, which is on *E Music*, though his name isn't in the liner notes due to an unfortunate printing mistake.

I took a deep breath as I sat in my office, looking through pictures of Tito, thinking about how his unique sound and dynamic style had inspired so many of us. When Coke and I were touring with Santana in New York, we took Carlos to the Corso Club to check out Tito. That's how Carlos came to record *Oye Como Va* and *Pa Los Rumberos*, both songs written by Tito. He had a style all his own. The sound of his timbales is what still stands out after all this time. You can hear just a few hits, and you know it's Tito–that short, precise hit with his very small timbale sticks. He played very staccato, very fast. Sometimes he'd use two or three sets of timbales: a regular set, a small set called "Timbalitos," and a large set called "Thunder Timbs."

Eventually, I let in the reality of his forever-absence. Tito was gone–my teacher, my friend, the only one I'd ever truly looked up to. He enriched my life with his amazing musicianship and his loyal friendship. He set a standard and a legacy for Latin jazz music. He's the real legend. The King of Timbales. My job, as I see it, is to keep doing what Tito, as well as Mongo, Cal, Willie, and the other greats, would be doing if they were still with us. I still want to experiment with new things and expand the genre–and I applaud the younger guys who are doing that–but I don't want to neglect my other mission: to preserve what my old friends were doing so well.

I'd wanted to be a bandleader and a musician like Tito, someone who played for the love of the music, not for the money or the fame. Sometimes when I'm on stage, hitting the timbales or stepping back to watch a band member solo, I'll feel him. His spirit is there with me, coming through me even. I bet he and Coke are having a ball up there. I like to think of them setting down the tempo, knowing I'll be up there to join them when it's my time.

The second major loss that year was my sister Alice. She had asthma for as long as I could remember, and she had been ill with various ailments for a while. Then she was diagnosed with cancer. The last time I saw her, I knew it would be the last time. There she was in her bed at her daughter Josie's house in Oakland. She was small, fragile, the light in her eyes dimming. She looked years older than she had the week before. The room smelled older too. It smelled like death. I gave her a hug, and she started crying. I pretended it was a hello-hug, but we both knew what it really was: a goodbye-hug. I tried to hide my tears to be strong for her.

Her kids were her sole concern. "Pete, I'm so worried about them." Her cries got louder. "I don't want to leave them," she said. "They need me." I wiped her tears. "They'll be fine, Alice. I promise." I didn't know what words could possibly provide the kind of comfort I so wanted her to feel.

"She's going to die really soon," I told Juanita as we walked away from Josie's that day. Her words were echoing in my head: "My kids need me." She had always been so intent on keeping her family together, a concern I understood well. It was probably the main reason she had stayed with her husband for so long. As a devout Catholic, who our sister Jay called "Sister Bertrille" (from *The Flying Nun*), Alice believed that keeping family united should be the primary goal. Even though her kids were all grown up, she needed to know I'd look out for them. And I assured her I would. Before driving away, Juanita and I prayed for her. As we drove back home, I found myself thinking back to our early days. She and Bobby had lived in Mexico with our grandmother, and so we missed out on time together. I wanted that time back, more time to make childhood memories, more time to grow up together. But of course, time is something none of us can get back.

Two days later, my dear sister, just one year older than me, was gone. She and I had already mourned the loss of Coke. She had been such a supportive older sister, always so proud of our musical aspirations, even helping me finance *Yesterday's Memories, Tomorrow's Dreams*. Now I could only hope she'd joined Coke in heaven. I had another angel watching over me.

༼ঙ༽

Losing Tito and Alice in the same year was devastating. When feelings of depression crept in, I tried to focus on work. Business at the club was steady, and I had every reason to predict that it would continue to go smoothly.

We had big crowds, great music, and a solid reputation within the community. One day, as I sat in my office reviewing the earnings from the night before, a detective from the Berkeley Police Department showed up. He let me know that for months now they'd been keeping a close eye on the owner, who'd been involved in illegal activity. They were just about to arrest him and would be putting a freeze on all his assets and holdings. The detective's advice was clear: Shut down the club and relocate before everything explodes. He warned me that my name would be in the news, and I'd be getting a lot of bad press. The club wouldn't be able to stay in operation since they'd be taking away his license. I looked around my office and then stepped out into the beautiful club, which had become a second home for us. *Everything can just change in a moment.* I'd have to say a quick goodbye.

Just a few days later, I met a woman who owned a place in Alameda called Spotlight on the Square. She asked me to check it out, as it had recently been remodeled. She'd heard through the grapevine that I was moving after doing well with the club in Berkeley, so she wanted me to partner with her in running this club. I liked that it was a lot bigger than Mister E's and it had a large parking lot and patio. It was also visible as soon as you entered Alameda from Oakland via the Alameda Tube Parkway. The only major project would be adding a stage. I had a good architect in mind. I was in. The move and advertising would have to start immediately. I booked Sheila and her band for the grand opening, and most of my old employees were ready to make the move with us. We called it "Mr. E's Spotlight on the Square." A new name, a new place, and a new partner.

I'd come to find out that legal partnership doesn't always mean harmonious partnership. From the beginning, my new partner and I just didn't see eye to eye. She thought that Sheila and her band should play for free since she was my daughter. She also didn't understand having to provide hotel rooms for the band members coming from L.A.

She didn't agree with expenses for things like advertising, costs of liquor, and employees. She saw large crowds and assumed that meant tons of net profit. She didn't think we were keeping accurate books, and she didn't trust Zina as manager. So she hired someone to watch our every move. Week by week, things got worse. It was time to get out, but dissolving our partnership meant bringing in lawyers to settle the big questions–who owns what, who owes what, etc. All of that led to arguments and resentment. The stress was too much for me. I finally gave up. I was out.

Meanwhile, our landlord had sold our home, and we got notice that we had two weeks to move out. I left town for work for two weeks, and when I returned, Juanita had already found us a new home: 1227 Pearl Street in Alameda. Somehow, Juanita managed to do all of the moving on her own. I didn't like the place, but Juanita had no choice but to grab the first good enough place she could find.

In the new year, January of 2001, I made a concerted effort to put the club business behind me. I was tired of trying to figure out why all my clubs had failed. It didn't help that an article in a local paper was exploring the same question: "Why can't Pete Escovedo keep a club open?" I eventually shook it off. I'd been down and out before, and I'd get through it.

I wasn't able to see any silver linings around all the clouds that kept rolling in. My brother Phil wasn't looking well. He'd been losing weight, and his complexion seemed to be getting more and more pale. He had always been a big, physically fit guy, but he was looking so small, and his energy seemed low. Even his playing was slower than usual. Whenever I asked how he was feeling, he'd say he was fine. He kept his health problems to himself for a long time, until he finally confessed that he'd been getting tested by doctors. He kept the test results to himself for a while before letting us know the truth: he had cancer. He told me not to worry. "I've had a good life, Pete," he said in his usual laidback voice. "I got to play music and enjoy my family. I'm okay with this." He seemed to have found peace with his illness. But I had not. Shortly after this conversation, on January 15, 2001, Phil's wife called to tell me he had passed away and asked if I wanted to see his body. As I went to say my final goodbye, I was heavy with regret. I should've checked on him more. I should've told him to take better care of himself. I was flooded with memories–the night he first introduced himself as our brother, the many stages we shared with Coke as The Escovedo Brothers, all the laughter, all the music. Phil was gone, and a piece of me was gone with him.

CHAPTER THIRTY

FLYING SOUTH

It was a hard time–the closing of another club, a rushed move out of a home we loved, and, most painful, the loss of Phil. I found myself yearning for change and seriously considering a big move. Sheila had been encouraging us to move to Los Angeles for a while. She wanted us closer to her, and she believed I'd have bigger and better professional opportunities down in Tinsel Town. It seemed like the Bay Area, as much as it was our home, wasn't able to offer as much as it used to in terms of good paying gigs in nice venues. I'd tried my best at running clubs, and I'd played in just about every club–from the little dives like the Shell by Grand Lake in Oakland, to the cozy spots like the Sweetwater in Mill Valley, to the grand venues like Davies Symphony Hall in San Francisco. It just felt like work was drying up, and I was caught in a déjà vu, round and round on the same circuit. I knew it was time to take my daughter's advice and open myself up to more opportunities.

So the next month, February of 2001, we finally did it. Juanita, Zina, and I packed up and caravanned down to sunny L.A where Sheila, Peter Michael and Patrice, and many of our grandchildren were already living. It was hard to leave Juan and his kids, Zeawnna, Brittney, and Juan Jr., but we knew they'd visit a lot, that Juan would be working in L.A., and that we'd be back to the Bay quite often. Still, driving away wasn't easy. The Bay Area is where I'd lived as a kid, cut my teeth as a musician, met my wife, raised our children, and welcomed our grandchildren. As we transitioned from the 580 freeway to the Interstate 5 South, I had to hold back some tears.

When we got there, our first mission was to buy a home. No more renting. We looked all around L.A. before finally settling in Valley Glenn. The moment we walked in, we knew it would be ours. The layout felt right, the street was quiet, and there was a pool. As we signed our papers with the real estate agent, I turned to Juanita, who was ecstatic. "We'll give it a year here," I told her. "And if it doesn't work out, we can always move back home." We've been there ever since.

It took a while for me to adjust, but Juanita and Zina eased right in. They liked the weather, the beach, and the overall vibe. It grew on me. It was great being near so many of my grandchildren, and I liked doing more studio sessions and gigs with Sheila and Peter Michael. I still missed the Bay. The good news is that, once I moved to L.A., I got called to work in the Bay Area more than ever before. I guess being an out of town artist made me more marketable, so I've been working there consistently ever since. Funny how things work out.

I figured the best way to get situated in L.A. was to do a new Latin jazz CD. That way I could keep myself busy with a creative project while also getting to know the good L.A.-based musicians. Sheila and I co-produced *E Music*, the most Latin CD I've ever done. This one turned out well, and it left me feeling more connected to the L.A. music scene.

It was revitalizing to work with some of the best musicians from Southern California. Peter Michael and Sheila played drums and percussion (Juan was on tour so he couldn't be on this one), and Ray Obiedo came down from the Bay to lend us his great guitar skills.

Being down south made it easy to participate in my brother Alejandro's project. He'd written all the music to a play, *By the Hand of the Father* (the music also on a CD of the same name that I recorded on), which was based on the life of Mexican families who came to this country in hopes of something better. Our own father's story was featured. In the summer of 2002, we performed the play at a museum in Long Beach. We also went to Austin, Texas, to perform on the television show *Austin City Limits*, where the actors performed in front of the band, and a big screen behind us displayed images of Mexican farmworkers with voice overdubs. When a photo of my father appeared, and we heard his booming voice, I had to hold back tears so I could focus on playing the song. I was overwhelmed by how much I missed him.

I'd been inspired by Alejandro's project, something really creative and outside the box, so when Concord contacted me about making another CD, one that had a different feel than the others, I was especially game. They suggested doing a live performance recording at a small club, which would be a new experience for me. We scheduled a two-night performance at Humphries in San Diego, California. There were a few technical challenges. Since the bandstand was so small, we had to put the horns in front of the rhythm section. The band was made up of L.A. and Bay Area musicians because I wanted a mixture of musical flavor. We did a second live session in Japan at the Blue Note.

Both sessions were great. I produced it with John Burk, and we decided to call it simply *Pete Escovedo Live*. I was proud of the record and continued to feel good about my partnership with Concord Records. That's why I never would've guessed that this would end up being my last recording with them. I got my release letter in the mail. Sales were slow, it stated, and they had to cut their Latin jazz roster down to just a few artists. I held the letter in my hands and read it a few times before calling Juanita over. As usual, she was reassuring. "It has nothing to do with how good the music is, honey." I wasn't sure what to think.

Now, whenever I hear that CD, I realize she was right. The music still sounds fresh and vibrant, and the recording quality is top notch. I've learned–often times the hard way– that music quality doesn't always determine sales quantity. Back then, I was pretty floored. *Should I shop for another label? Should I just keep trucking along and see if any offers come my way?* I prayed on it, asking God to show me the way. Prayer, as it had done countless times before, led me to keep working hard and to let my passion for music guide me.

CHAPTER THIRTY-ONE

SUNRISE

I didn't have time to sulk about *Pete Escovedo Live*'s lackluster sales since the next few years brought extensive international tours and lots of local performances and gigs–Guatemala, Japan, Cabo San Lucas, and back home to the Bay Area for many shows in between. I celebrated my birthday in July with shows at Yoshi's in Oakland, which had become a tradition. I was blessed to perform a tribute to Tito Puente in Los Angeles and Dallas with an orchestra from Puerto Rico, do a live recording with many great musicians for Don Grusin at Platinum Live in L.A., play at the New Orleans Jazz Festival, and perform as a special guest at the GRAMMY's party with Poncho Sanchez and Dave Valentin. The family also got to appear in the film *Chasing Papi*. Things were sailing along, and life felt wide open and fun. I was fulfilled by performing with my kids and other talented artists, as well as by family time with the ever-growing Escovedo clan.

And then I was dealt an unexpected blow. On February 15, 2004, I got the news that my father, Pedro Escovedo, passed away in his nursing home in Chula Vista, California. He was 96 years old. He lived a long and full life filled with many ups, many downs, many hardships, and many loves. Even after all he put my mother through with his drinking and self-destruction, she always loved him. Even though he was not anywhere near a "perfect" father, I always loved him too.

I was grateful for the time I'd had with him as an adult. We made many good memories, like those at the annual gathering of the entire Escovedo family in Rosarito Beach, Mexico, where we celebrated Dad's birthday. It was a three-day party full of food, drinks, and of course, music. I was one of the pallbearers at his funeral, and in his honor, we all sang that song my father loved the most: *Solamente Una Vez*. "Only once I loved. Only once and never more..."

My father's death is something I'm still working out for myself. I wish I had more time with him. So many years gone by that will never be again. The reality of death, the inevitability of it, is something I struggle with in quieter moments. I just haven't been able to fully accept it, though I've long tried.

C3❧80

I did my best to stay busy. Music, as always, provided solace. I played with Ray Vega's band at Yoshi's in Oakland and in Monterey. I participated in a tribute for Victor Pantoja, who was fighting cancer. I recorded with my brother Alejandro. I closed out the month of March and filled most of April with gigs in the Bay Area. In May, I traveled to Malaysia to play a private corporate event. I got to visit the tallest building in the world and somehow found the nerve to walk across the glass bridge that connects its two towers. The view was stunning, but I'm not a huge fan of heights. Louis Fasman, the trumpet player in my band, joined me for some golf with the gentlemen in charge of the event. I didn't play well, but at least I got to say I played golf in Malaysia.

I was back in the Bay Area, playing in San Jose for their Music in the Park event, when life took another turn. Thousands showed up for the show, their largest turnout ever. And that got me thinking. Maybe I wasn't completely done with being a club owner. Maybe my next club venture could be in San Jose. I did an informal poll right there on stage. "What do y'all think of me opening up my next club right here in San Jose?" They went crazy. I looked around at the band. They were flashing me smiles and giving me the "thumbs-up" sign. Why not give it a go? I'd done it before. I had someone who had expressed interest in partnering. There was no competition since San Jose didn't have any live music jazz clubs. I began my search for the right location. Since the word was out, lots of calls started coming in from realtors and investors.

I contacted the architect who had handled the remodeling in the Alameda club, and we partnered up. When we heard about a rock club that was going out of business on the corner of South First Street, we headed over there to take a look. It was pretty dirty and messed up, but I could see the potential. There was a large stage, a dance floor, and enough room to add dressing rooms, offices, and a VIP area upstairs. I also liked that it was visible from all sides of the streets. We negotiated a deal that would enable us to lease the building at a reasonable rate. Both the purchase of the liquor license from the previous owners and the cost of remodeling was on us. We each put up $50,000 to get the project rolling. And so there I was: another club, another city, another gamble, another life change.

As the renovations came along, I still had gigs to play. I was back at Yoshi's in Oakland for my birthday, where I got to announce to the audience that I'd be opening up a new club. Things were moving fast. The club was looking polished–new bar, tables and chairs, carpet, offices, dressing rooms, bathrooms, and P.A. system. The new marquee was up, announcing the opening of the Pete Escovedo Latin Jazz Club. My favorite part was the Rat Pack room, decorated with photos and memorabilia of Frank, Sammy, Dean, and Marilyn. The club was a first-class entertainment venue. My dream had come true, again.

We started out with a bang, opening on July 21 and 22 with a grand open house that allowed folks to check out our new space. Sheila and her band gave an amazing performance as the opening band on July 23 through 25. My Latin jazz orchestra played July 30 through August 1. It was good timing since the annual San Jose Jazz Festival had brought thousands of music fans to San Jose. I featured local jazz groups all weekend, and the club was packed.

Juanita and Zina held down the fort while I was traveling and fulfilling previous gig obligations. Soon we were back home in Los Angeles, leaving my partner in charge. Everything seemed to be running smoothly. I was back and forth from L.A. to San Jose every week. Juanita and I celebrated our 48th wedding anniversary, but we didn't get much of a chance to pause and give it too much attention since the club was getting more and more consuming. By fall, the schedule was taking its toll. My expenses for flights and hotels were mounting as well. We decided to fix up one of the rooms upstairs, so I could stay there and use the shower attached to the dressing room. The club literally became my home away from home. We were getting great feedback from bands and music-lovers in San Jose and surrounding areas, but we were still having trouble breaking even.

I tried for a while to save it, but nothing was working. My partner decided to get out first. He closed out the whole operation, including the bank account. I had to reopen all the accounts–electricity, phones, water, bank, garbage, and deliveries. It was a mess. I was continuing to pour my own savings into the club, but week after week, we sank more and more into debt. I was becoming a nervous wreck. People weren't coming to the club as much as they used to. Even the best bands weren't drawing, but I never stiffed them. I always made sure they were paid. I'd been in the other position too many times–playing gigs and then being told by the venue that the check was in the mail. Too often, those checks never came.

In a last-ditch effort, I borrowed some funds and stayed open a few more weeks. But it was a lost cause. I'd read this kind of writing on the wall before. Sometime early in the new year, I decided I had to close the club. I can't remember the exact date. I guess some dates you'd rather not lock in your memory.

The owner was kind enough to let me slide on the rent until I could sell the place. I even gave up some of my paintings to cover the rent. Eventually, a group of young men offered to buy the place, with the intention of turning it into a dance club. I sold them the club with everything in it–all the remodeling, all the beautiful furniture, all the love. They got it for half of what I paid for it. I paid off all my debts, packed up my personal belongings, and left San Jose with my head down and without a dime in my pocket. That was another hard blow. Confronting another failure was tough. My dream of becoming a club owner had been realized multiple times, but my dream of becoming a successful club owner just wasn't meant to be.

◆◆◆

The first few months of the new year were pretty slow, which was just as well. I needed time to rebound. Soon work picked up again. I was off to the New Orleans Jazz Festival, Miami, New York, and various gigs in the Bay. I celebrated my 70th birthday at Yoshi's in Oakland, per usual. The place was packed with family and friends. Our Bay Area gigs, particularly those in Oakland, felt like family reunions and parties. Sometimes I was surprised to get a pay check because I'd had so much fun playing and catching up with everyone. There's just no love like Bay Area love. The following month, the city of Los Angeles paid tribute to me at the Ford Theatre in Hollywood. It was great to play with the band that night, and of course to be joined on stage by Sheila, Juan, and Peter Michael.

In September, I got news of another death. We lost Ed Kelly. He was the one who invited me to join his little Latin jazz group in high school. He knew how eager I was to get started in music, and he gave me that opportunity. We'd stayed close ever since.

When I got back home from playing in Italy with Sheila, Juan, and my orchestra, there was more sad news: Manny Duran, the original piano player for Cal Tjader, passed away. In the early days, Coke and I had worked with him and his brother Carlos for many years. Hearing about the passing of yet another influential musician really threw me. I continued to go about my days and my gigs, but grieving all of these losses felt unbearable.

I did my best to manage. Thanks to God, my family, and my music, I was able to focus on all my blessings and move forward, despite the grief that took over whenever a memory of a lost loved one would flash across my mind. The next few years were busy—playing with my orchestra all over the U.S. in places like Washington D.C., the ALMA Awards dinner, Austin with Alejandro, the Hollywood Bowl, Yoshi's, and the Dolores Huerta concert at the Greek in L.A., where Carlos Santana joined us. We caught Sheila with Ringo Starr's band in Vegas. A wonderful highlight was my 50th wedding anniversary with Juanita. We celebrated at Sweet's Ballroom in Oakland—the same place where Sheila, at the age of 5, joined me, Phil, and Coke on stage to "sit in" with the Escovedo Brothers. (Her "sitting in" was actually standing in, since she had to stand on a chair in order to reach the congas with her little hands.) We rang in 2006 playing at the Fairmont Hotel in San Francisco.

CRUD

The first loss of the next year was Ray Barretto. I'd long admired Ray's talent and vision. He took a chance on changing his musical style. He'd been known as a salsa percussionist, so when he started his own Latin jazz band, the audiences were shocked. I was there when he did his first performance with his new band, opening for a salsa group, and the crowd actually booed him. But he was unstoppable. He was following his heart. He was just so ahead of the game, and he went on to make some great records with his Latin jazz band.

I thought back to a time when I invited him to play at my San Jose club. He'd turned it down because he thought he couldn't fill the place. "I'd do it for you, but I'm afraid you'd lose money."

"But everybody loves you," I said.

"Your club is too big, Pete. People aren't coming out to hear live music the way they used to."

It was a rude awakening. The club across the street with a D.J. was always packed; but clubs with live music–even clubs booking living legends–were struggling.

CHAPTER THIRTY-TWO

SOMEDAY WE'LL GET BY

In the fall of 2007, after winding down from some great travel and shows–playing with Prince in Las Vegas, having a great run at Yoshi's in Oakland for my birthday, and doing some jazz festivals in St. Lucia, Atlanta, and Hollywood and Highland–I found myself longing to revisit the music that still held such an important place in my heart. So with the idea in mind of recording a live DVD in Los Angeles, I began calling all the original Azteca band members. Most of them seemed as excited as me: Lenny White on drums, Paul Jackson on bass, Bill Courtial on guitar, Errol Knowles and Wendy Haas on vocals, Victor Pantoja on congas, and Jules Rowell on trombone. I brought in some of my current band members as well: Murray Low on piano, Melecio Magdaluyo and Alex Murzyn on saxophone, and Mario Gonzales on trumpet. My kids would be joining me as special guests. As I walked into the first day of a four-day rehearsal, I was flooded with emotion. Seeing all the old guys in the same room again moved me. And the fact of Coke's absence hit me hard.

I'd love to say that the rehearsals were a dream, but they were more of a nightmare. So many disagreements and frustrations. Fortunately, we managed to put our egos aside and focus on what mattered most: the music. What bittersweet songs–each one a reminder of the guys who'd passed away, each so clearly missing the nuanced sounds only my brother Coke could've provided. But the music united those of us blessed enough to still be standing, those of us who still had the privilege of playing notes, singing melodies, strumming strings, and making beats. The gig was special.

The recording itself, however, was not–lots of technical, sound, camera, and lighting issues. And the mix was neglected. Much to my disappointment, it was released anyway. At least the heartfelt interviews made it into the DVD. It's a shame, though, that the power of the night didn't translate onto film.

When I was asked to put the Azteca band together again for a San Francisco concert benefitting autism awareness and research, I had to think about it. Preparation had been a headache last time, even though it was so great to reconnect as friends and musicians. I'm always honored to be a part of a benefit concert. Next to working with underserved youth, it's my favorite way of giving back. So I rolled up my sleeves and got to work. For this gig, it was Curtis Ohlson on bass, Victor Pantoja on congas, Bill Courtial on guitar, Jules Rowell on trombone, Louis Fasman on trumpet, Melecio Magdaluyo and Justo Almario on saxophone, Sheila on drums, and three Azteca originals on vocals: Errol Knowles, Wendy Hass, and Linda Tillery. The band felt great, but the logistics left something to be desired. Since we had only one day to rehearse, we couldn't set up the stage the way I wanted, given all the other bands in the lineup and the limited time for transition between them. Plus, the sound and P.A. system were horrible. We still did our thing, and the crowd seemed to like it. After our performance, Carlos Santana presented Sheila and

Linda with a Women of Latin Rock award. Before handing the award to Sheila, he said some very nice words about me and Juanita. He mentioned the influence I had in Latin music and the influence she had in being the heart and soul of our family. It had been years since I'd played in Santana, and it always feels good to reconnect with Carlos now. He will eternally be an important part of the Escovedo family's musical history.

CHAPTER THIRTY-THREE

ALL AROUND

After reconnecting with Azteca again, I realized it was time to revisit another project that I'd dreamed about for a long time: recording with the E. Family. We'd talked for years about each of us participating equally on the same CD, all of us signed on one label, and then getting to produce, write, and record our own family CD. We'd performed together since the kids were, well, kids, but we hadn't managed to record a collective project. Finally, in 2008, our intentions and schedules aligned. A relatively new company liked the idea of recording the first ever E. Family record and signed us immediately. We asked some of our good friends to join us on the project: Earth, Wind & Fire collaborated on two songs, Gloria Estefan and Wes Quave did a great duet, Raphael Saddiq and George Duke played on a soulful tune with Joss Stone, Israeal Houghton did a new version of his beautiful gospel song *All Around*, and Prince performed piano and vocals on a song he wrote for Sheila called *Leader of the Band*. You can bet that with four Escovedos in charge, each song was as percussion-heavy as possible. We also gathered as many Escovedos, Garderes, and Chevereses as we could in an L.A. studio to participate in a special bonus track and film. It was a family reunion and a musical celebration. Two of Peter Michael's sons, Dominic and Peety, were featured in several songs, Zina sang the bridge on *I Like It*, and Juanita played the guiro in perfect time.

For three months, we worked steadily, making sure everything was just right. We spent day and night in the studio, playing, writing, laughing, debating. There were some heated negotiations about arrangement, about how things should be mixed, and about who plays what. We weren't used to sharing the leadership. We'd all played on each other's projects, but now, who's the boss? I'm the Dad, but my kids had become pros in their own right. We were creatively, financially, and legally equals on this project. Through it all, there was an undertone of collaboration, fun, and deep gratitude for getting to turn this family dream into a reality.

When the CD was finally finished, we couldn't stop playing it, and we couldn't wait for the public to hear it too. That's when we learned that the record company was folding. They were out of money, and so our labor of love sat on a shelf. The sense of defeat didn't last long. Sheila negotiated a deal to buy the masters so she could release the CD on her own label, Stiletto Flats. We called it *Now & Forever*.

Promoting and touring was so much fun, a dream come true to be on the road with my kids, performing this fresh new music after having finally made our first E. Family record. In January, 2009, Sheila and Juan opened and signed the first box of CDs at the NAMM music convention in L.A. We sold out shows, and our new songs got great reception. The hometown crowd at Oakland's Yoshi's went wild. The first single, *I Like It*, was the number one requested song on local radio station KBLX, and the love we felt at home was as solid as ever. We played throughout the states and internationally as well.

⊂⊃⊃

Between E. Family gigs, I went out with the Latin Jazz All Stars, all musicians from New York except me. Jason Franklin, a promoter from Georgia, put the group together with the makeup of the band varying somewhat from gig to gig, depending on our availability. I've always been honored to be included with them, most often playing with Claudio Roditi, Ray Vega, Dave Valentin, Chembo Coronell, Junior Terri, Arturro O'Ferrel, and Steve Turre. It's both challenging and rewarding for me–the one guy from the left coast always trying to keep up with these legends.

There's always been a distinction between East Coast and West Coast playing. I was lucky that when I was coming up, a lot of East Coast musicians came to play in California, so I learned to integrate their style into my own. But there's just no mistaking a musician *from* the East Coast who's influenced by the music of Cuba and Puerto Rico and can play with that straight-ahead style. West Coasters were fed so many different styles of music, so our sound is more of a mixture. But East Coast groups like the Fort Apache Band or artists like Ray Barretto they play the real Latin jazz stuff, and there's nobody in the Bay Area that plays like that.

Right before I go on stage with the Latin Jazz All Stars, I usually start second-guessing myself. "Am I good enough to hang with these guys?" They never rehearse. An hour or two before we go on stage, we just write out the set list. For some reason, it always works out. It's a true ensemble, and we improvise well together, the horn players giving us chords, and all of us communicating through eye contact and gestures, like touching the top of our heads to indicate "back to the top." Every time I play with them, I learn something–how they prepare in sound check, how they improvise and communicate musically during the show, and what they share during post-gig meals about the trials and joys of living and breathing music day in and day out.

So along with the occasional Latin Jazz All Stars gigs, the usual Pete Escovedo Orchestra gigs, and now all the E. Family shows, my schedule was packed. The calendar said I was 73, but my schedule said I was 23! When the family and I attended the wedding of Kendra Wilkinson and Hank Baskett at Hugh Heffner's Playboy mansion—we'd grown friendly with them since they filmed their reality show across the street from our home—I was one of the few guests with a head of white hair. I couldn't complain. More white hair and wrinkles meant I was blessed enough to keep aging and keep living.

ଔଋ

The hard part is that as you live longer, you'll inevitably experience more loss. That summer I got news that Richard Lewis passed away. He had been in the Carlos Federico band—my very first professional gig at Oakland's California Hotel when I was 19. Later that year, we lost Willy Vargas, the timbale player whose place I took in that same Carlos Federico band. Then we got the news that Michael Jackson died. I attended the moving funeral service, overwhelmed by yet another legend's passing. Sometimes on a day off, in a quiet moment in my office, at the golf course, or by the pool sipping a late morning coffee, I'd be struck by the magnitude of these losses. It can hit you like a freight train, when you stop to think about all those people who take their final breath and are suddenly gone.

I tried to remember to let the losses serve as a reminder of how precious each breath is. They taught me to be grateful for each and every opportunity. In October of 2009, I was given an opportunity I never would've imagined. I had the great honor of performing at the White House for President Obama and his family. We performed on the White House lawn for *In Performance at the White House: Fiesta Latina*. (I joked it was the only time they'd let Mexicans on the lawn who weren't there to trim the grass.) Sheila was musical director for the event, and she did an extraordinary job. I was a proud Daddy indeed. I joined her on stage–double the timbales–for a rendition of Tito Puente's *Oye Como Va/Ran Kan*. It felt like we had Tito's spirit up there with us–Tito hangin' at the White House with his old friend and his goddaughter. It was great having the Obamas on stage with us during the last song. We gave Malia and Sasha drumsticks, and they joined us on the timbales. After the show, Sheila and I met with the President and First Lady. After posing for photos and engaging in a warm exchange with the Obamas, Sheila and I held hands and had to suppress the urge to skip out of the White House's reception room like giddy children. "Sheila, we're a long way from 9th Ave. and East 21st Street," I told her. "Look how far we've come." She nodded, all smiles. "I know, Pops. And you paved the way." I began laughing, remembering President Obama's cool vibe and swagger. "That guy seems like he's from Oakland. Our president is cool. I think he's an Escovedo."

The rest of the year flew by–TV performances with The E. Family, gigs in the Bay Area and beyond, and New Year's Eve at a club in L.A. that Sheila co-owns, The Conga Room. The E. Family brought in the New Year like we always do, with lots of percussion and lots of prayers for peace in the next year.

2010 was smooth sailing at first. There was lots more E. Family touring and promotion–like the NAMM show in L.A., Anthology in San Diego, Jazz Alley in Seattle, RAZZ Room in San Francisco, and a Cinco De Mayo concert with Poncho Sanchez back in L.A. Then, on March 12, I got news of another loss: My dear friend Victor Pantoja passed away. Victor had played with Willie Bobo for many years, and of course with Azteca. He was one of the family's closest friends, and I took the news of his death pretty hard.

In July, I turned 75. Wow. 75 and still around. Thank you, God. The shows kept coming–E. Family, my orchestra, Latin Jazz All Stars, and sitting in as a guest with various bands. For her birthday in September, Juanita and I enjoyed a quick San Diego getaway, just the two of us. We walked along the water, ate in Little Italy, and went to a few night clubs. Our 54th wedding anniversary came the next month, so we took off for another getaway, this time to Vegas. The rest of the year I continued to perform with the family and with my orchestra, mostly in various California venues. Zina turned 43 in November, and Sheila turned 53 in December. What happened to my little girls? "We're still your little girls, Daddy," they told me when I raised the question. I rang in New Year's performing for my loyal fans back in San Jose.

The beginning of 2011 was busy. After some shows in San Diego and San Francisco, I flew with the family to Japan to play at the Cotton Club and the Blue Note for five show-days and one day off. Two of Juan's children, Juan Jr. and Brittney joined us, as did Juan's wife, Sarah, and my dear friend and manager, Victor. After one day off back at home, we were out again to play at Dakota's Jazz Club in Minneapolis. Minneapolis feels like a second home, since Sheila lived there for a while, Prince lived there, and our close family friends, the Davisons, are there as well. Next, we were off to Denver and then Detroit. After all that travel, it was great to be home at the end of January. There's nothing like relaxing at home when you feel like you've earned it. For me, the best kind of relaxation is enjoying meals with the family, watching late night black and white movies, and spending time by the pool or on the golf course.

The following month, the E. Family played at Yoshi's in San Francisco. It was a fun show, though it felt strange to play without Juan, who had gone back to Japan to play with Jody Watley. After that Yoshi's gig, Sheila went straight back to her hotel and started to write her memoir. (Her book, *The*

Beat of My Own Drum, has now been published. It took a lot of courage to share what she did–to put it all out there. Based on the comments I've heard, and the tears I've seen from readers at her book signings, I know Sheila's book is making a huge difference for people. I couldn't be prouder.) Juan joined us for the Jazz Alley shows in Seattle and Sheila performed with Prince a few nights at the end of the month. Juan and Carlos Santana joined Sheila on stage with Prince in Oakland for a Latin number. After some days preforming in Cabo San Lucas, Mexico, the E. Family opened for Prince at the L.A. Forum. The E. Family kept pushing along–a great show at L.A.'s Greek Theatre and a performance on George Lopez's show.

In spring and summer, I got to play for some wonderful charity events. A highlight was participating in the San Leandro High School music program with Sheila. The family and I are passionate about this cause–keeping arts and music in public schools. I always made it a point to bring the kids along to benefits when they were little–especially those supporting young people–and now I get to share the stage with him at these important events. Sheila is so committed to providing art and music education to underserved youth that she cofounded two foundations devoted to this very cause, Elevate Hope and Elevate Oakland. I think back to my time in school and at the orphanage. Without art and music, my spirit would've diminished, probably beyond repair.

CHAPTER THIRTY-FOUR

THE E MEDLEY

Between E. Family and Pete Escovedo Orchestra gigs that summer, I began preparing for my art show, which would coincide with the usual birthday run at Yoshi's in Oakland. I'd had art shows in Alameda, San Francisco, and Los Angeles, but never before in Oakland. We had lots of help from friends, who loaded up the art and merchandise in Los Angeles and then unpacked it all in Oakland at a nice space in Jack London Square right across the street from Yoshi's. We had enough room to hang my paintings and display smaller items like hand-painted instruments and Zina's shadow boxes with Escovedo memorabilia, vases, and CDs. Everything looked great and made for the perfect after-party space.

The club was buzzing. All the shows were sold out, and we had a lot of fans excited about The E. Family's hit single, *I Like It*. Each night, I'd announce the art show at the gig, and then after the second show it seemed like most of the audience followed us into the gallery until the wee hours of the night–sipping wine, viewing and purchasing art, and having great conversations about music and life (the two being interchangeable for me, of course).

Another great part of that week was filming an E. Family documentary. We toured Oakland, visiting all our old homes, the kids' schools, and the sites of my old clubs. The kids pointed out where they got into their first playground fights, where Juan and Peter Michael burned down the garage, where Sheila was a proud traffic guard in grade school, where the kids were caught smoking a cigarette behind the house on E. 21st Street, and where Zina would sit and enjoy the sunshine on the front stoop. It was amazing to literally revisit the landscape of so many family memories. It was a journey back in time, a reflection of all the joy, the struggles, the births, the deaths, the love, and, of course, the music. The experience was also a beautiful celebration of where we are today, who we've become, what we've accomplished, and what we stand for as a family. Our E. Family CD title says it all: *Now & Forever*.

After the last show on Sunday, we were all pretty wiped out. We had a late-night bite at Home of Chicken and Waffles, and went straight to bed since we had to get up early the next morning to break down the art show. Family and friends came and helped us load up the van and clean up the place. Then my small band and I headed over to Santa Cruz for a performance at the Kuumbwa Jazz Center. I always enjoy playing with my small band. This one featured Roger Glenn on vibes and flute, Ray Obiedo on guitar, Murray Low on piano, Marc van Wageningen on bass, Peter Michael on drums, and Juan on congas. We don't ever rehearse, and our sets aren't as demanding or as intricate as an E. Family show. We play a lot of standard Latin jazz tunes and some originals by Ray and Roger. It was fun and low-key, a great way to close out a hectic week. We made it home, unloaded the van, and then returned it to the rental site. We said good night to our friends and crawled into bed. What a beautiful week–a birthday I'll always remember.

The rest of the year, the E. Family band stayed busy with gigs and TV appearances throughout the U.S. We also got the chance to participate in some great benefit concerts too, for Delancey Street and Glide Memorial Church in San Francisco and CARRY in Beverly Hills.

Juanita and I made time to celebrate our 55th wedding anniversary with a getaway to Palm Springs. We reminisced about our first time in Palm Springs together, when Juanita brought Juan and Sheila so we could all be together for Christmas during my first time gigging away from home. And there we were again, alone this time, celebrating over five decades of partnership. We had grown children, grandchildren, and great-grandchildren. Sometimes, when we allow ourselves a little time to reflect, we realize that life is but a dream.

CROW

The preciousness of life is only made clearer every time someone I know loses theirs. When someone in your family passes away, your life as you know it changes forever. When I got news of another family member's death, my life not only passed before me, but seemed to be fading away. On December 6, 2011, my younger brother Bobby suddenly passed. He had a very different life from mine. He was the apple of my grandmother's eye, while I was a reminder of my father, a man she detested. He was raised in Mexico, while I was raised in the Bay Area. And Bobby was never told "no." In other words, he was spoiled. When he moved to the U.S., back to Pittsburg, California, he could hardly speak English. He didn't get to spend much time with our mother and father, and I think he craved time with them. As he grew older, he wanted to join Coke and me in the music biz. He made his living as a bartender and auto salesman, but his eyes lit up when he saw us performing on stage. He loved to sit in, play timbales, and act as unofficial stage manager. "I'm not a musician," he'd say. "I'm an entertainer." And that he was. He greeted folks with a big hug, he laughed and smiled big, and he took great pride in the family's accomplishments. He might have been one of my biggest fans. Bobby married four times, never to find the perfect mate. He had three children: Rene, Tara, and Arianita. Like Coke's son, Paris, Bobby's son, Rene, has become a great professional musician. Paris' daughter, Melody, is a great singer, and Rene's son, Cameron, is proving to be a great drummer in his own right. I like to think that they're living out Coke's and Bobby's dreams.

Unfortunately, like my other brothers Coke and Phil, Bobby had a drinking problem. It saddens me to think about his sudden death and his unfulfilled musical dreams. I realize now that I should've helped him more. But I can't bring those days back. Lord, how I wish I could. We paid tribute to Bobby's life at a memorial in Oakland. That's what he wanted—no funeral, just a celebration with music, family, and friends. The place was packed. I managed to pull myself together and get back to work soon after the memorial. I had a show at the RRAZZ Room and then celebrated Sheila's birthday during her performance at Yoshi's in San Francisco. The shows were great, but I was distracted. Thoughts of all the family that I'd lost kept drawing me inward: my mother, my father, Alice, Bobby, Coke, and Phil. Their memories and spirits are still in my mind, heart, and soul. But I miss them being right here with me, in the flesh. Often, when I lie in bed at night and my waking thoughts are drifting into dreams, I have vivid images of each of them. I hear their voices. I see them as they once were. And when I wake, I miss them even more.

CHAPTER THIRTY-FIVE

FLYING EASY

The year ended with a last-minute trip to Vegas, where we visited Chris Angel for some dinner and some magic. It felt strange not working on New Year's, but it was nice to relax and enjoy a mini-vacation. My heart had been pretty heavy with grief, and I needed some time to reflect.

Back to business in 2012, but it wasn't business as usual. This new year started out with a new creative adventure. The Cupertino Inn, in the heart of the Silicon Valley, commissioned me to do enough paintings for three suites, which in and of itself was an exciting task. Then they asked if I would do new paintings for over 30 rooms–four to five paintings for each room. I couldn't believe they wanted so many rooms filled with my artwork. My first challenge, aside from figuring out how I'd make the time to do so much painting, was to decide on what to actually paint. Some people have noted that my work can be pretty emotional, intense, or even dark, and I surely didn't want to give any hotel guests nightmares from staring at my paintings. I wanted the imagery to be soothing, or at least emotionally neutral. I decided to paint within four series-themes: Flamenco, Springtime, La Peña, and Jazz. It took me over a year to complete. The hotel was really pleased with the paintings, and I was really proud to have accomplished such an out-of-my-comfort-zone task. Now I tell people that if they want to spend the night with Pete Escovedo, they just have to book a room at the Cupertino Inn.

In January, after Peter Michael and I drove up from L.A. to the Cupertino Inn to deliver some pieces, we were off to San Francisco for a run at Yoshi's with my Latin jazz orchestra. I'd really been looking forward to this gig and playing my stuff again. As much as I love playing with other bands, and of course playing in the E. Family band with my kids, there's nothing like *my* good ol' Latin jazz. Then I was off with Juan and Peter Michael to play at San Diego's Anthology–a nice club with great sound. It was fun to have my boys with me, and we had a great time exploring the beauty of San Diego during the day. Our friend Loni Love was performing nearby, so she and our friend Rosa hung out with us during the day. We didn't get to see each other's shows, but we got the personal Loni Love comedy show, which always means good fun and laughter.

I returned home and rested up for a bit before flying to Seattle for a three-night run at a cool jazz club called Jazz Alley. It's a spot where the audience really appreciates live music. During the day, Juan and Peter Michael and I did a clinic at a music store called Drum Exchange. We told stories from the road, gave advice to musicians, and demonstrated some rhythms. It became a fun jam session, with kids and kids at heart all joining in. The owners were extremely nice folks, and the turnout was great. Juan and I flew back to Los Angeles, got off the plane, and went directly to rehearsal with the band Sheila put together for an Indonesia event the next day. After a long rehearsal, we got back to the house, unpacked, and then repacked. Then we were off. Nineteen hours and one layover later, we landed in Jakarta,

Indonesia. Not an easy trip, especially since I developed a fever somewhere along the way to Taipei.

But the show must go on. The first show went well, and I gave it my all. But the next day I was exhausted. So rather than exploring Jakarta and catching up with friends who were playing the festival (Herbie Hancock, George Duke, Al Jarreau, Dave Koz, Ron Carter, Poncho Sanchez, Erika Badu, Bobby McFerrin, Manhattan Transfer, and others), I had to stay in my hotel room all day and try to get better. I was coughing, sneezing, and my fever was running high. A doctor visited my room, told me I had a bad case of the flu, and prescribed some medication. I managed to make it through the second night's show, but by the time we flew home the next day, I was in bad shape. I went straight to the doctor, who told me I had walking pneumonia. It took me two weeks to fully recover. When people tell me they envy my world travel, I tell them that short international trips aren't always what they're cracked up to be.

Once I was better, Peter Michal and I drove up to the Bay for a bunch of events we had planned. First stop was Santa Clara College and then a benefit for St. Jude's Children's Hospital at the RRAZZ Room. We had a great time with the RRAZZ Room owners, Robert and Rory, and enjoyed watching and hanging with all the great performers on the bill, including Deana Martin, Mary Wilson, Edna Wright, Freda Payne, and CeCe Peniston.

A highlight of this trip up north was getting to do a drum clinic for some kids at Seneca Family of Agencies, a wonderful nonprofit organization where Juan's wife, Sarah, works. The kids were slow to warm up to us, but once we brought out the percussion bag and showed them a few things, and after I told them about my time in a similar group home as a boy, they were eager to join in. Each grabbed an instrument, and we had a big jam session. We taught them some beats, and they taught us some raps and dance moves. The staff thanked us for spreading some joy, and we thanked them for letting us meet these amazing kids. We left much happier than when we arrived. There's nothing like sharing music with kids. It's something I'd been doing with my children ever since they were old enough to tag along. I'd load them and all our percussion instruments into the car and visit various children's facilities. We'd get the kids on shakers, tambourines, and bongos and try to give them a glimpse of the joy that music can bring. "Take us home with you," they'd beg as we packed up our bags. Sheila, Juan, Peter Michael, and Zina would be so sad as they looked out the windows, watching the crying kids waving goodbye. It was hard explaining why we couldn't take them with us.

Things stayed busy. Juan and Peter Michael and I were invited to record on El Chicano's new record, which was a great honor. They are an important part of Latin music history. I used to be booked with those guys a lot back in the day, and it was fun to reconnect. We recorded at a cool studio once owned by the Jacksons and later bought by the House of Blues. We then headed back up north to play a benefit for Lincoln Child Center in Oakland and then, when Sheila returned from Europe, we played the Playboy Jazz Festival with her band at the Hollywood Bowl. I turned 77 on July 13, and this time instead of playing at Yoshi's, we celebrated with a show at Spaghettinni's in Seal Beach. We recorded my next CD, *Live from Stern Grove*, before another whirlwind of shows–Detroit, San Diego, Livermore, San Rafael, Los Gatos, and then a recording session for dear family friend Raphael Saadiq back home in L.A.

While resting on a day off, I got a call from Michael Wolf, a piano player who played with Cal Tjader back in the day. Michael told me he wanted to put a band together to pay tribute to Cal. He explained that we'd be playing at the Monterey Jazz Festival as well as some other gigs around the Bay Area. Juanita and I drove to Monterey for a day of rehearsals at Clint Eastwood's golf course. Later that night, we played at a private party Clint hosted, and then the Cal Tjader tribute band played for Monterey Jazz. It was wonderful to play Cal's music again and to celebrate his life and his work through those great tunes.

I had a few days off at home before hitting the road again–The E. Family played at A&T in North Carolina, where we were welcomed by their amazing drumline. Next we were off to Seattle for another run at Jazz Alley. We then joined Sheila in Las Vegas, where she and her band were performing for the Obama campaign, helping to bring out the Latin vote. We got to visit with the President for a bit after her show, which is always a huge pleasure.

I spent Thanksgiving with Juan and my band in Cancun, Mexico, where we played a three-day jazz festival. The stage was set up right on the beach, and people from all over the world came to see many great artists. The weather was perfect–sunny with a warm breeze. *Viva Mexico*. We made it home in time for Zina's 45th birthday. Sheila turned 55 the following month. What a blessing to see my girls grow into such extraordinary women.

Another sad note at the end of this year: We lost another dear friend and a very talented musician, Paul van Wageningen. He was such a kind soul, who played in my band for many years. Juanita and Juan and I attended his memorial in Oakland. His brother, excellent bassist Marc van Wageningen, along with Paul's beautiful wife and family, got lots of support that night–so many friends who gathered to play music and celebrate Paul's too-short life.

C≥∞

And as always, the loss was not far from another performance–this one was New Year's Eve at Yoshi's in our hometown of Oakland. And so another year in my life came to an end. Only time will tell how many years there'll be ahead of me. I'm thankful for every moment I have. I've been around the world, witnessed many things, met many people, experienced many soul-moving connections, endured many hardships, and learned many lessons. I've been blessed with the gifts of family and music, two things that I've had the privilege of experiencing hand in hand. I can only live each day with great gratitude that God has given me such a rewarding journey.

CHAPTER THIRTY-SIX

LORD REMEMBER ME

My faith in God has not always come easy to me. I suppose my relationship with him continues to evolve. I was baptized Catholic, and the Catholic Church was always in the background of my childhood. Church on Sunday. No meat on Friday. I had baseball games on Saturday, so if I'd had even a bite of meat on Friday, I'd worry, assuming God would punish me by making me play badly or causing me to lose the game. *I'm going to let down the whole team*, I'd say to myself as I walked onto the field. *Why did I eat that burger last night?*

I elected to be an altar boy in Saint Mary's grammar school. I was incredibly dedicated to that role and even thought about becoming a priest. It was a thought that made sense to me since I was so devoted to mass and to my altar-boy duties. And it was a thought that kept me close to my mom. She was very Catholic, and our regular church attendance meant a lot to her. That dependable timeout from regular life–a hard life, full of stress related to money and my father and needy kids—must have provided a nice respite for her. It was a place to renew, exhale, and pray for change. Becoming a priest seemed like the most prestigious thing I could achieve within the church. I wanted to be important and, more than that, to make my mother proud.

As I grew older, my devotion to the church lessened. I'd think about the nuns at Saint Vincent's, the ones who would slap our hands and the back of our heads, the ones who would punish us rather than console or counsel us, and I had trouble believing that their God—any God—would condone treating kids that way.

Juanita's family was probably stricter Catholic than mine. After we married, and I made music my main focus, she and I gradually let go of a strict adherence to religion. We took our kids to church on Sundays and prayed as a family, but we gradually got disillusioned with the rules. We lost the connection. The seemingly unanswerable questions of faith kept gnawing at me. Later on, when the kids were grown, we reconnected with church. Peter Michael and Sheila became devout Christians and got very into The Bible as the word of God. Their passion was contagious. Juanita and I renewed our connection to religion, but this time it felt more like a connection to spirituality—less about following rules and avoiding punishment and more about a personal relationship with God. This relationship has gotten stronger, and while I don't believe in any religion per se, I do call myself a Christian. I feel free to think and act according to my own autonomous choices.

While my faith feels more natural, more in line with an authentic spiritual connection, I can't say that I'm at total peace with regard to faith and religion. I still have a lot of questions. Sometimes they keep me up at night: *Where does God come from? How did He get here? How is He the one that started the universe and created this world? Why did He make Adam and Eve sin? Why is the world full of sin? If I go to heaven, will I see my parents and friends? Are heaven and hell real? Why do some people, like terrorists, kill for their religion?*

I've had long conversations about all these questions of faith—with my family, with pastors, with atheists, and with agnostics. So far, my questions and their answers haven't brought me any lasting satisfaction. Sometimes I feel like going to church with Juanita, who goes every Sunday. I take in the sermon and feel nourished by it. I pray there with passion and conviction. Other times, I just don't feel like going. Recently, we started going back to a Catholic church. The vibe of being in a real church, instead of just a building, has been refreshing. I believe, and yet so many things confuse me. I believe in science and evolution too. So how can I put this all together in a way that truly makes sense to me?

I wonder how much my confusion is wrapped up in a fear of mortality. I know this body of mine is going to stop. It has to. There's a beginning and an end. Wouldn't it be nice if we got to pick an age and just stay there? I'd like to hang out in my 50s forever. Those were the best times. I wish I didn't have to die and leave all of this, missing out on being with my family, my grandkids, my great-grandkids, my great-great-grandkids, and so on. Some people have tried to reassure me that I'll get to see it all from up above. But I'm not so sure. I guess that's where faith comes in. It's a leap of faith I don't always know how to take.

CHAPTER THIRTY-SEVEN

I LIKE IT

2013 was feeling as busy as 2012. I performed at the opening of the San Francisco Jazz Institute in January of 2013 with Bill Cosby and John Santos, and then I was off to do some shows in Japan. For the next few months, I played gigs all around the Bay Area.

As I thought about my upcoming July birthday gigs in Oakland at Yoshi's, I realized it was time for a change. I was yearning for some of the music from the good ol' days–my good ol' days–so I decided to bring some Azteca music into the show. The lineup was great: Murray Low on piano, Marc van Wageningen on bass, Ray Obiedo on guitar, Sheila on drums, Louis Fasman on trumpet, Joel Behrman on trombone, Melecio Magdaluyo and Alex Murzyn on saxophone, Juan on congas, and Peter Michael, Alysha Antonino, and Leah Tysse on vocals–13 musicians for my birthday on July 13 in the year 2013. That was one of the best and most enjoyable performances of my career–doing the music of Azteca again with my three kids playing beside me as I celebrated 78. That music both reflects and ignites something deep within me. I hope to record some more of it sometime soon.

୧୫୨୦

We lost another dear friend the following month: George Duke. Sheila was just 18 when George called her to join his band and go on the road. I could give my blessing because I knew George would look out for her. "Don't worry, Pete," he said. "I'll keep the hounds away." He was a great man, a great talent, and yet another great loss in my life.

୧୫୨୦

In September, after celebrating Juanita's 76th at Morongo Casino in Cabazon, California, I set out for a new adventure: Dave Koz's Jazz at Sea European Cruise. I knew that Dave had planned a special trip, and I was looking forward to spending some time with him. He's an extremely talented musician and a good friend. I like to say that he's my only Jewish son, and I'm his only Mexican father.

We left for London, and then from there we were off to Rome. I wanted to see the Colosseum first as I'd missed it back when I was in Rome with Santana. Our private tour guide filled us in on all the history. I couldn't believe we were standing where gladiators battled to their deaths, and where Christians and slaves had to fight lions, and usually lose, for entertainment. I flashed back to movie scenes–Charlton Heston, Kirk Douglas, Richard Burton, and Victor Mature in roles set there. This enormous structure was a sight to behold. I took a moment to look up to the sky, sending out a "Thank you" to God for allowing me the opportunity to witness such an important piece of historical architecture, the largest amphitheater ever built. I got to stand there amongst all that magnificence. Me. Little ol' me, the guy who still sometimes feels like that bad kid cutting school, or that little boy waiting for his mom to keep her promise.

We caught a cab to the Vatican, where our guide was from Pasadena of all places. I was mesmerized by his stories about the history, the Pope, and the enormous wealth of the Catholic Church. But nothing compared to seeing Michelangelo's work in person. It was so much more stunning than it is in books. After walking through the rooms and halls filled with exquisite statues and tapestries, we finally reached the Sistine Chapel. As we walked in, I thought of Charlton Heston again, playing Michelangelo. We all looked up, not saying a word, taking in the beauty of his paintings–each section telling a story of mankind and God. The beginning of life and the spiritual beginning of humanity. It felt like time had stopped. In this silent room, I felt the presence of God.

Next we went to St. Peter's Church where we got to see the remarkable altars, and all the statues of Christ and the saints. On the way back to the hotel, I couldn't get myself to join in on the conversation. I'd been rendered speechless, so moved by what I'd seen and by the very opportunity to see it.

The following day we were up early to board the ship. My body clock was turned around, and I hadn't slept well. So I ordered room service and got myself packed. After having coffee with Sheila in the lobby, we checked out and boarded the bus that would take us to the ship's port. There were many great musicians on this trip: Michael McDonald, Gerald Albright, Keiko Matsui, Peter White, Mindy Akbar, Brian Colberson, Larry Graham, Kirk Whalum, and a lot of talented backup artists from all over. Man, what a lineup. We were able to bring some of our band members: Joel Behrman on trombone, Alex Murzyn on saxophone, Raymond McKinley on bass, and Mike Blankenship on piano. We all arrived at the dock and went through the process of checking in on the Navigator of the Sea, a Royal Caribbean cruise ship. After setting sail, we settled into our cabins and then joined Dave on deck so he could introduce us to the passengers. Off to Messina, Sicily, we went. The movement of the ship lulled me to sleep.

The next day we caught a bus to Taormina, a small town that sits on top of a cliff overlooking the sea. There were a lot of small shops and cafes lining cobblestone streets. We spent over three hours walking around and then stopped at a jazz club inside a hotel nestled on the side of a cliff. After heading back to the bus and boarding the ship again, we cruised all day to Mykonos, Greece. I had breakfast with the gang and then did my scheduled interview with Larry Graham and Ralph Harris. It was called "Just Us Guys." After the interview, I went off to sound check as this was our night to perform. The first show's crowd wasn't that energetic, and the sound was off, so I left feeling a little disappointed. But the second show was much better, maybe because the crowd was more jazzed. Sheila played great, as usual. The next day I felt like I was coming down with something, so I decided to rest up as much as I could. I guess my life on the road, or in this case on the sea, wasn't as wild as it once was. Naps have now become a requirement. After we arrived in Mykonos, I had an interview with Taliyah, a DJ from The WAVE radio station in Los Angeles. This one was billed as "Pop the Cork with Pops." Translation: Free champagne with yours truly. While Sheila and the gang went ashore for some sight-seeing, I stayed on board to nurse my cold and enjoyed seeing Keiko Matsui and Gerald Albright on my cabin television.

We arrived in Athens the next morning and got to enjoy a full day off. One of the largest ports in Europe, Athens is a large city with a lot of hustle and bustle. Our tour guide pointed out the huge structures that had been built for the Olympic Games. We arrived at the bottom of the Acropolis and walked all the way up to the top of the mountain to see the stunning structures up close. We had to stop and catch our breath a few times along the way because it's a pretty steep walk. At the top, the historic ruins, the proximity to the Parthenon, and the view of the city made the hike well worth it. Later, at the plaza filled with rows of shops and restaurants, we gave ourselves a lunch break at an outside café, where a group of Greek musicians played for tips. Sheila took the tambourine from one of them and started playing it, then ran around the restaurant collecting tips for the band. After that, she started a big jam session. The patrons and the band got a real kick out of it. My daughter, the ham. Like mother, like daughter. Soon it was time to get back to the ship for that evening's entertainment portion, a Motown review, with each artist performing a song. We chose *Don't You Worry 'Bout a Thing*. It was great fun. A lot of artists dressed in a toga outfit for that night's costume theme. Of course, I chose to stay in my suit and tie. I gotta be me.

As we set out for Naples the following day, I dug into the many delicious food choices. I probably ate too much, but oh well. It was a vacation with pay. Why not indulge? Sheila and I had a fun time leading a drum circle by the pool–getting the passengers to participate and letting them pick up instruments and play along with us. It ended up turning into one big conga line around the pool, with everyone singing to the beat of the drums. Later, it was "Formal Night," so you know I enjoyed dressing up for that one. Not too much of a stretch from my normal attire. I put on my tux and was dressed to impress.

As soon as we arrived in Naples, we immediately took off to explore, walking around the main shopping area, eating lunch, and buying a few things for folks back home. We went back to Rome and then boarded the bus to head back to the airport. Homeward bound. It was so nice to be greeted by Juanita and Zina at the airport. Sheila usually prefers to arrange a car service, but her budget-conscious mama always insists on picking us up, no matter the time of day or night.

I rolled down the window and took a deep breath. One never knows how these trips will pan out. This one was special, and I was grateful to have been a part of it. The cruise, the talented artists, the music, the Colosseum, the Vatican, the Sistine Chapel, the metropolis. It was a rich and fulfilling trip. *Thank you, God, for this opportunity*, I thought. *Thank you for giving me such a wonderful life.*

CRBO

A few days later, I was back to the local grind. I drove up to the Bay Area with Peter Michael, where we played with Juan at Angelica's in Redwood City. The following night, I played a fundraiser in my hometown of Pittsburg, raising money for the high school's marching band. I'm honored to have my name on one of the seats in the Pittsburg High School auditorium. (I like to say I have an honorary Ph.D.–a Pittsburg High Doctorate.) For the last song, we brought them all up to join us. Bringing kids on stage and leaving them with the memory of performing with my band continues to be one of my favorite parts of the job.

Later that month, I flew back east with Sheila and her manager, Gilbert, to perform a series of concerts with a Smooth Jazz lineup. The concerts were a lot of fun, and the audiences loved our show. That's always a great feeling. We returned home on October 21, just in time for Juanita and me to celebrate our 57th wedding anniversary.

There always seems to be that constant juxtaposition of celebration and grief. We got word that Mary, mother of Peter Michael's wife, Patrice, had passed away. We went back to the Bay Area to attend the service. It was a beautiful and emotional service. I had a hard time believing Mary had passed–another loss that was hard to comprehend.

After the service, Juan drove back to Los Angeles with us since the E. Family was receiving a Los Angeles Jazz Society award in Beverly Hills. It was the second official award the E. Family had received, and we were honored by this recognition of our contribution to the industry. Louie Cruz Beltran introduced us, and it was moving to be there with my kids in the company of jazz greats. We ended the night with a performance, complete with a friendly solo competition of sorts, trading 8's–my kids and I each making a statement, daring each other through our rhythms. Our playing says, "Let's see what you can do! Top that!" I'll tell you, they keep me on my game. When they wow the audience with their quick-as-lightning rolls and impeccable chops, I like to tell the audience, "I taught them everything they know." But the truth is, we're teaching each other. The communication and interdependency of percussion is amazing. When I'm engaging in that magical musical conversation with my family, there's just nothing like it in the world.

Sheila was off for Hawaii the next day and later for Europe, where she'd be promoting her new CD. In the meantime, Peter Michael and I were back to the Bay Area again for an NAACP gig before a quick turnaround back to L.A. for Tommy Davidson's and Sinbad's birthday parties.

Sheila got home on Zina's 46th birthday, and we celebrated with a quiet dinner at her favorite restaurant. Sheila would turn 56 the next month, celebrating at Yoshi's again. Zina and her best friend, Courtney, opened the show with their Morris Day and the Time lip sync number. Juan also did a great opening percussion segment with his friends James Henry, Tony Flores, Kenny Blackman, and his son, Juan Jr. rapping. It was a fun birthday show for Sheila. Her band sounded great. I couldn't get over my daughters' ages. It was all moving way too fast for me.

Time marches on. When I look through all the calendars I've preserved through the years, I see all the gigs as well as all the birthdays, the anniversaries, the deaths, and the friendships made and lost. So much time, and yet all of it seems to have gone by in a flash. Sometimes I wonder if I've lived my best life. Have I given enough love? Have I acknowledged my mistakes and learned from them? A person's life is so short, even when lived to old age. How much more time do I have?

I feel good and my health is good, thank God. So I'll just keep trying to maintain it. When the day comes that I feel I can't do it anymore, or my playing gets sloppy and I can't keep up, that's when I'll know it's time to stop. I hope that day never comes, but I know it will. Until then, the beat goes on.

CHAPTER THIRTY-EIGHT

HELLO LIKE BEFORE

December 31, 2013 at the San Francisco Jazz Center was sure to be a great gig. It was their first New Year's since they'd opened just a few months prior. It's always fun for the family and me to celebrate in the Bay Area, particularly in a beautifully designed venue like this one. Unfortunately, Sheila was booked at Walt Disney Hall in Los Angeles, and Zina had to stay in L.A. for work. I did have by my side Juanita, Peter Michael and his wife Patrice, Juan and his wife Sarah, as well as family friends Moms and Pops Gumbs, and the rest of the Bay Area band, which is, to me, family. The place was packed—every seat sold. We rang in the New Year in typical Escovedo fashion, playing our hearts out on stage and leading the countdown for the audience. Between songs, we'd reach down to our glasses, tucked next to our instruments, to steal sips of champagne. Juanita came out on stage for the countdown, gave me a kiss as the clock struck midnight, and then grabbed a guiro for the next song. (She's more of a ham now than she was when we were kids. I call her "Lucy" because, like Lucille Ball, on *I Love Lucy*, she always has to get in on the act. The crowd can't get enough of her.) After our kiss, I turned around to do an air "cheers" to my sons and bandmates. I sent out a silent "Happy New Year's" to Sheila and Zina, and to all my beloved family and friends. Before launching into the next song, I looked up to God, thanking him for yet another year.

I counted in the band and then allowed myself to get swept away by the music, those sweet sounds of Latin jazz that have been the background of my life, interwoven into every moment of happiness and pain. As I struck my timbale sticks onto my well-worn drum heads, I looked out into the audience, making eye contact with some in their seats and some on the dance floor. They were covered in glitter, moving and grooving, bouncing balloons across the room, hugging and kissing, blowing their kazoos, and beaming with joy. I wondered what unexpected hardships the next year would bring for all of us. I wondered what blessings were in store. *This moment in time is worth celebrating*, I thought. *This moment in time is enough.*

ENCORE

After doing some painting in my garage-turned-art-studio, I'm back in front of my computer which is splashed by light from the bright winter sun coming through my office window. Juanita is pitter-pattering about the house as usual–cleaning, singing along to the gospel music channel, and periodically checking on the overflowing pot of gumbo, which will be more than enough to feed us tonight and to feed the many unexpected visitors who'll undoubtedly be stopping by this week. I guess you could say we've got an open-door policy.

I've just now gone through all the pages that constitute this book, my story. I've spent many days and nights putting my life onto these pages. I've shared a lot, key moments in my development as a musician, an artist, a husband, a father. I haven't told everything–a few things remain too sacred to share with the world–but I've told what makes sense to tell.

Even though I've covered events from my birth to the present moment, I keep wondering if I'm done. Have I

269

remembered enough? Have I shared all the significant parts? And, most important, did I put down in writing what's in my heart and soul? Those might be unanswerable questions. I suppose "done" is subjective. So I guess I'll go with my gut on this one.

This process, while sometimes great, has at certain points along the way moved me to deep sadness, like when I was forced to realize how few stories I have about my parents. I'm sorry I missed out on a stronger relationship with each of them. I longed for more closeness with them, for a more stable home life, and for the kind of guidance I imagined other kids got from their parents. I was on my own in many ways, following the music and paving my way, sometimes a solo act in search of a band.

My music dream led me to create that band, that family, a home within the music itself. And ultimately, the music led me to a real family of my own, as God blessed me with Juanita and our children. With the wondrous creation of this family, I've more than made up for gaps in knowledge about my parents and for a sometimes broken connection to my family of origin. I was shaped and, ultimately, deeply fulfilled by this search for family. The music was this search's soundtrack.

I have an extraordinarily devoted and supportive wife, magnificently loving and talented children, grandchildren, and great-grandchildren who bring ever-expanding happiness and peace to my heart. They are constant reminders that I must've done something right. What more could this guy ask for?

And so this book ends. I hope there's another one to follow, another performance, another song, another roll of the sticks, another encore, and another day with *mi familia*. I hope there are many more beginnings in this life...this melodic life in the key of E.

Pete Escovedo
December 24, 2016
10:14 a.m.
Valley Glen, California

The end.

The kids (Peter Michael, Juan, Sheila, and Zina) with Juanita and me at our 60th wedding anniversary and vow renewal (October, 2016)

© Rony Armas

E. FAMILY SHOUT-OUT

Juanita, a.k.a. "Moms": She's one of a kind. They really broke the mold with her. I feel so blessed that we've chosen to spend our lives together. What a lucky guy I am to have found her, to have chosen her, and to have received her amazing love for so many years. She said "yes," and for that I'll be forever humbled. I couldn't have created this life with anyone but her. She's been there every step of the way, cheering me on through all the trials and all the joys. And we're still together. We're still finding out things about each other, which keeps our love fresh. She keeps surprising me with her quirks, her jokes, her thoughts, and her infinite capacity to love–with a fierceness–those lucky enough to know her.

Sheila: She's the most talented person I know. She's so committed to excellence, which makes her persistent, uncompromising, and passionate. She just doesn't settle, and I respect that so much. She'll go out of her way to help and uplift her family, her friends, and anyone in need. Her commitment to helping youth makes me especially proud. She's forever the big sister, forever the first born. She's a magnificent woman and forever my little girl.

Juan: He's become such an extraordinary musician. I look up to him and truly admire him for how hard he's worked to become so great. He's also always working on becoming a better man–always seeking, learning, growing. He's faced many challenges with courage, humility, and strength. He's so devoted to family, and he has a huge and generous heart. I'm so very proud of all he's accomplished–professionally, musically, but most of all, personally.

Peter Michael: He's one of the kindest people I've ever met. He's always fun to be with and talk with. He has a great mind, great spirit, great talent, and a great personality. He's a wonderful family man and a strong man of God. He's pretty darn close to perfect.

Zina: She's in her 40s but always our baby. I hope and pray that she'll one day be 100% free from the disabling anxiety that has plagued her. I'm so proud of how hard she's worked on herself, how brave she's been. She'll never give up. She deserves total freedom and happiness. What a beauty, inside and out, always so attuned and sensitive to others' feelings and needs. She has great ambition and passion, so I know she'll achieve all her goals.

MY ANGELS, MY LEGACY

Children

Sheila Cecilia Escovedo	December 12, 1957
Juan José Escovedo	March 13, 1959
Peter Michael Escovedo	July 7, 1961
Zina Ann Escovedo	November 26, 1967

Grandchildren

Reco Jerome Escovedo	August 28, 1978
Nicole Camille Madden	September 21, 1981
Zeawnna Escovedo	June 24, 1981
Brittney Escovedo	November 6, 1985
Peter Michael Escovedo IV	November 18, 1982
Juan Jr. Escovedo	March 1, 1988
Brendon Salvador Escovedo	September 28, 1984

Dominic Alexander Escovedo	April 15, 1990
Patrice Arianna Escovedo	September 22, 1994
Sidena Anastasia Escovedo	September 22, 1994
Evan Pearson Escovedo	December 28, 2014

Great-Grandchildren

Reco Jerome Escovedo Jr.	October 14, 2008
Taleia Elizabeth Escovedo	March 30, 2000
Jaidyn Brandon Escovedo	August 23, 2001
Tamiko Kyla Escovedo	January 25, 2002
Tamya Nanice Escovedo	February 11, 2005
Brendon Salvador Escovedo Jr.	December 3, 2006
Peter Michael Escovedo V	December 12, 2006
Kylan Michael Escovedo	July 11, 2007
Harlow Winter Kate Madden	January 11, 2008
Kingston Elijah Escovedo	January 31, 2009
Sparrow James Midnight Madden	September 9, 2009
Hendrix Moreau Escovedo	September 10, 2014

VENUE SHOUT-OUT

Venues are my homes away from home, where I can lose myself in music, collaborate with great musicians, and give the audience, and sometimes myself, a much needed escape. Since the stage is where I've lived so much of my life, I'm compelled to acknowledge the venues I've found most rewarding. Most of these spots are still up and running, though some are long gone. Here they are, in no particular order: The Hollywood Bowl in Los Angeles, California (Playboy Jazz Festival); Blue Note Jazz Clubs in Japan; Monterey Jazz Festival; Yoshi's Jazz Club in Oakland and San Francisco, California; Jazz Alley in Seattle, Washington; *Fiesta Latina* at the White House with President Obama; Ford Theatre in Los Angeles, California; Dave Koz Jazz at Sea Cruise; Cancun Jazz Festival in Mexico; Detroit Jazz Festival; San Jose Jazz Festival; Aruba Jazz Festival; Chicago Jazz Festival; RRAZZ Room in San Francisco, California; New Orleans Jazz Festival; Salt Lake City Jazz Festival; Dakota Jazz Club in Minneapolis, Minnesota; Mister E's

Club in Berkeley, California; Disney Hall in Los Angeles, California; Greek Theatre in Berkeley, California; Greek Theatre in Los Angeles, California; Anthology Club in San Diego, California; Concert by the Sea in Redondo Beach, California; Sweets Ballroom in Oakland, California; Jakarta Jazz Festival in Indonesia; Keystone Corner in San Francisco, California; Stern Grove Festival in San Francisco, California; KJAZZ Hollywood and Highland in Hollywood, California.

PETE ESCOVEDO'S ALBUMS

Azteca's *Azteca* **(1972)**: George DiQuattro (clavinet, acoustic piano, keyboards); Coke Escovedo (timbales); Pete Escovedo (percussion, vocals); Bob Ferreira (saxophone, flute, piccolo, wind); Wendy Haas (vocals); Tom Harrell (trumpet); Paul Jackson (bass); Errol Knowles (vocals); George Maribus (electric piano); Mel Martin (flute, piccolo, saxophone, wind); Flip Nunez (organ); Victor Pantoja (congas, vocals); Rico Reyes (vocals); Jules Rowell (trombone); Neal Schon (guitar); Jim Vincent (guitar); Lenny White (drums)

Azteca's *Pyramid of the Moon* **(1973)**: John Brinck (drums); Bill Courtial (guitar); George DiQuattro (piano, clavinet); Coke Escovedo (timbales); Pete Escovedo (percussion, vocals); Bob Ferreira (saxophone, flute); Wendy Haas (vocals); Tom Harrell (trumpet, flugelhorn); Paul Jackson (bass); Tony Juncale (bass); Errol Knowles (vocals); George Maribus (piano); Mel Martin (saxophone, flute); Mike Nock (synthesizer, piano); Flip Nunez (organ); Pat O'Hara (trombone); Victor Pantoja (congas); Rico Reyes (vocals); Thomas Rutley (bass); Neal Schon (guitar); Lenny White (drums)

***Solo Two* (1977)**: Alvin Batiste (clarinet); Al Bent (trombone); Billy Cobham (drums); Willie Colon (bongos); Pete Escovedo (timbales, vocals); Sheila Escovedo (congas, vocals); Roger Glenn (flute);Tom Harrell (trumpet); Abraham Laboriel (bass); Ray Obiedo (guitar); Julian Prester (trombone); Mark Soskin (keyboards); Bill Summers (percussion), Pablo Tellez (bass)

***Happy Together* (1978)**: Billy Cobham (drums); Tom Coster (keyboards); Pete Escovedo (percussion, vocals); Sheila Escovedo (percussion, drums, vocals); Eddie Henderson (flugelhorn); Randy Jackson (bass); Mel Martin (saxophone); Ray Obiedo (guitar); Mark Soskin (keyboards)

***The Island* (1983)**: Tim Acosta (trumpet); Jorge Bermudas (percussion); Carl Carwell (vocals); Daryl Coley (vocals); Lynn Davis (vocals);); George Duke (keyboards); Juan Escovedo (percussion); Pete Escovedo (percussion and vocals); Peter Michael Escovedo (percussion); Sheila Escovedo (percussion, drums, vocals); Roger Glenn (flute); Hans Halt (bass); Richard Kermode (keyboards); Ray Loeckle (saxophone); Dave Mathews (keyboards); Ray Obiedo (guitar); Louis Olds (trumpet); John Rae (vibes); Claytoven Richardson (vocals); Scott Roberts (percussion); Jules Rowell (trombone); Larry Schneider (saxophone and flute); Linda Tillery (vocals); Marc van Wageningen (bass); Paul van Wageningen (drums); Wayne Wallace (keyboards, trombone)

***Yesterday's Memories, Tomorrow's Dreams* (1985)**: Jon Bendich (congas); Clifford Brown, Jr. (Master of Ceremonies); Sheila E. (congas, vocals); Pete Escovedo (vocals, timbales); Peter Michael Escovedo (drums); Dave Goldblatt (keyboards); Dave Mathews (keyboards); Marvin McFadden (trumpet); Ray Obiedo (guitar); Bill Ortiz (trumpet); Dan Reagan (trombone); Ismael Rodriguez (vocals); John Santos (vocals, bongos, batá, percussion); Norbert Satchel (saxophone, flute); Marc van Wageningen (bass); Paul van Wageningen (drums); Wayne Wallace (trombone)

Mister E **(1988)**: David Belove (bass); Jeff Cressman (trombone); Sheila E. (congas, vocals); Juan Escovedo (percussion); Pete Escovedo (timbales, vocals); Peter Michael Escovedo (percussion, vocals); Mike Galisatus (trumpet, flugelhorn); Robbie Kwock (trumpet, flugelhorn); Melecio Magdaluyo (saxophone, flute); Rebeca Mauleón (piano, keyboards, vocals); Vicki Randle (vocals); John Santos (percussion); Dan Shea (keyboards); Ed Smith (drums); Paul van Wageningen (drums); David Yamasaki (guitar); Wayne Wallace (trombone)

Latina Familia–Tito Puente, Pete Escovedo, and Sheila E. **(1989)**: David Belove (bass); Sheila E. (percussion); Jody Ente (vocals); Juan Escovedo (percussion); Pete Escovedo (percussion); Robbie Kwock (trumpet); Melecio Magdaluyo (saxophone, flute); Rebeca Mauleón (keyboards), Bill Ortiz (trumpet); Tito Puente (percussion); Claytoven Richardson (vocals); John Santos (percussion); Paul van Wageningen (drums); Wayne Wallace (trombone); David Yamasaki (guitar)

Flying South **(1995)**: Francisco Aguabella (batá, drums, percussion); Gerald Albright (saxophone); David Belove (bass); Jeff Cressman (trombone); George Duke (keyboards, piano); Sheila E. (shekere, congas, drums); Juan Escovedo (bongos, congas, percussion); Juanita Escovedo (guiro, percussion); Pete Escovedo (timbales, vocals); Peter Michael Escovedo (percussion); Louis Fasman (trumpet); Nikita

Germaine (vocals); Dave Gregoric (trombone); Lalah Hathaway (vocals); Robbie Kwock (trumpet, flugelhorn); Murray Low (keyboards); Dave Mathews (piano); Melecio Magdaluyo (saxophone); Rebeca Mauleón (piano); Harold Muniz (batá); Najee (saxophone); Andy Narell (steel pans); Ray Obiedo (guitar); Pastiche (vocals); John Santos (batá); Norbert Satchel (flute); Dan Shea (keyboards); Marc van Wageningen (bass); Wayne Wallace (trombone); Marty Wehner (trombone); David Yamasaki (guitar)

E Street (1997): Gerald Albright (saxophone); Al Bent (trombone); Howard Cespedes (saxophone, flute); Jeff Chimenti (piano); Jeff Cressman (trombone); Sheila E. (drums, percussion, vocals); Steve Erquiaga (guitar); Juan Escovedo (congas, bongos); Juanita Escovedo (guiro); Pete Escovedo (drums, percussion, timbales, timpani, vocals); Peter Michael Escovedo (drums, bongos, percussion, vocals); Louis Fasman (trumpet); Mike Galisatus (trumpet); Dave Gregoric (trombone); John Handy (saxophone); Derek Jones (bass); Robbie Kwock (flugelhorn, trumpet); Murray Low (piano); Melecio Magdaluyo (flute, saxophone); Dave Mathews (piano); Buddy Montogmery (vibes); Alex Murzyn (saxophone); Renato Neto (piano); Ray Obiedo (guitar, synthesizer, strings); Bill Ortiz (trumpet); Brenda Roy (vocals); Marc van Wageningen (bass); Paul van Wageningen (drums); Wayne Wallace (trombone); Van Waller (cabasa, tambourine, cymbal); Marty Wehner (trombone); John Worley (trumpet); The Revival Center Ministry Choir, Ron Cooley (director) and Regina Littlefield (conductor)

E Music (2000): Justo Almario (flute); Oskar Cartaya (bass); George Duke (piano); Sheila E. (drums, percussion, vocals); Pete Escovedo (timbales, percussion, vocals); Peter Michael Escovedo (drums, percussion, vocals); Ramon Flores (trumpet); Renato Neto (keyboards); Ray Obiedo (guitar); Joe Rotondi (piano); Francisco Torres (trombone); Ray Vega (trumpet); Arturo Velasco (trombone)

Whatcha Gonna Do (2001): David Belove (bass); Joe Bendich (congas); Clifford Brown, Jr. (Master of Ceremonies); Jeff Cressman (trombone); Sheila E. (congas, vocals); Juan Escovedo (bongos, percussion); Pete Escovedo (vocals, timbales, percussion); Peter Michael Escovedo (vocals, drums, percussion); Mike Galisatus (trumpet, flugelhorn); Dave Goldblatt (keyboards); Robbie Kwock (trumpet, flugelhorn); Melecio Magdaluyo (saxophone, flute); Dave Mathews (keyboards); Rebeca Mauleón (vocals, piano, keyboards); Marvin McFadden (trumpet); Ray Obiedo (guitar); Bill Ortiz (trumpet); Vicki Randle (vocals); Dan Reagan (trombone); Ismael Rodriguez (vocals); John Santos (vocals, bongos, batá, percussion); Norbert Satchel (saxophone, flute); Dan Shea (keyboards); Marc van Wageningen (bass); Paul van Wageningen (drums); Wayne Wallace (trombone); David Yamasaki (guitar)

Pete Escovedo Live! (2003): Justo Almario (flute, saxophone); Sheila E. (drums, percussion, vocals); Juan Escovedo (congas, vocals); Pete Escovedo (timbales, percussion, vocals); Peter Michael Escovedo (percussion, vocals); Louis Fasman (trumpet); Ramon Flores (trumpet); Mario Gonzales (trumpet); Dave Gregoric (trombone); Errol Knowles (vocals); Robbie Kwock (trumpet); Murray Low (piano); Melecio Magdaluyo (saxophone); Raymond McKinley (bass); Joe Rotondi (piano); Marc van Wageningen (bass); Paul van Wageningen (drums); Arturo Velasco (trombone); Wayne Wallace (trombone); Toshi Yanagi (guitar)

The E. Family's Now & Forever (2011): Alex Al (bass); Justo Almario (saxophone); Michael Angel (guitar); Jeff Babko (keyboards, organ, piano); Philip Bailey (vocals); Edward Brown (keyboards, organ, piano); Damon Castillo (guitar, keyboards, organ, piano, vocals); Kenneth Crouch (keyboards, organ, piano, vocals); George Duke (piano);

Larry Dunn (keyboards, organ, piano); The E Family—Sheila, Juan, Peter Michael, and Pete Escovedo (drums, timbales, percussion, bongos, congas, vocals); Randy Ellis (saxophone); Dominic Escovedo (vocals); Patrice Escovedo (vocals); Peter "Peety" Escovedo (rap); Zina Escovedo (vocals); Michael Esner (guitar); Gloria Estefan (vocals); Ramon Flores (trumpet); Frank Fontaine (saxophone); Mario Gonzales (trumpet); Cat Gray (keyboards, organ, piano); Israel Houghton (vocals); William Hogans (saxophone); Ralph Johnson (timbales); Lynn Mabry (vocals); Raymond McKinley (bass); Ray Monterio (trumpet); Greg Moore (guitar); John Paris (drum, guitar); Wes Quave (vocals); Joe Rotondi (keyboards, organ, piano); Humberto Ruiz (trombone); Raphael Saadiq (vocals); Garret Smith (trombone); Sy Smith (vocals); Ramon Stagnaro (guitar); Tim Stewart (guitar); Joss Stone (vocals); Marc van Wageningen (bass); Arturo Velasco (trombone); Verdine White (bass); Reggie Young (trombone)

Live from Stern Grove (2013): Michael Angel Alvarado (guitar); Joel Behrman (trombone); Sheila E. (congas, vocals); Juan Escovedo (congas, percussion, vocals); Pete Escovedo (timbales, vocals); Peter Michael Escovedo (drums, vocals); Louis Fasman (trumpet); Mario Gonzales (trumpet); Dave Koz (saxophone); Kerry Loeschen (trombone); Melecio Magdaluyo (flute, saxophone); Ray Obiedo (guitar); Joe Rotondi (piano); Arturo Sandoval (trumpet); Marc van Wageningen (bass)